This book is dedicated to Dr. Steven Clemants.

Healthy Soils for
Sustainable Gardens

Niall Dunne
Editor

Elizabeth Peters
DIRECTOR OF
PUBLICATIONS

Sigrun Wolff Saphire
SENIOR EDITOR

Steve Clemants
Craig Cogger
SCIENCE EDITORS

Joni Blackburn
COPY EDITOR

Elizabeth Ennis
ART DIRECTOR

Scot Medbury
PRESIDENT

Elizabeth Scholtz
DIRECTOR
EMERITUS

Handbook #192

Copyright © 2009 by Brooklyn Botanic Garden, Inc.

All-Region Guides are published three times a year by Brooklyn Botanic Garden, 1000 Washington Ave., Brooklyn, NY 11225.

Subscription included in Brooklyn Botanic Garden subscriber membership dues ($35 per year; $45 outside the United States).

ISBN 13: 978-1-889538-46-4
ISBN 10: 1-889538-46-9

Printed by OGP in China.
♻ Printed with soy-based ink on 100% post-consumer-waste recycled paper.

Cover and above: Healthy soils supply air, water, and nutrients that allow plants like the tomato seedling on the cover and the onion seeds above to grow into strong, vigorous plants.

Healthy Soils for Sustainable Gardens

Introduction

Niall Dunne

Plants are homebodies: They like to stay put and—in most cases—upright. A deep, healthy soil helps them accomplish this by anchoring their root systems. Soil provides other vital services to plants in addition to structural support. Most notably, it supplies plant roots with a source of air, water, and nutrients and insulates them from extreme temperature fluctuations. It's no exaggeration to say that a healthy soil is crucial to the health of plants—and by extension, all life on earth.

But what exactly is healthy soil? Until recently, a soil's health was measured mainly in terms of its physical and chemical properties: its texture, structure, pH, mineral content, and so on. Today, attention has shifted to include something else as well: the ecology of the soil. Soil is a habitat for countless organisms, from microscopic fungi and bacteria to larger creatures such as earthworms and millipedes. And we now know that these organisms—and the organic matter that sustains them—are key to the long-term fertility and viability of soil.

A healthy soil is also one that is not eroded, exhausted, or polluted. Modern industrial society has taken a heavy toll on the planet, causing large-scale habitat destruction, extinction of species, overexploitation of natural resources, and pollution of the environment—and soil has not escaped this abuse. Poor agricultural and horticultural practices such as over-tillage have led to widespread soil degradation. By one estimate, for example, human activity has increased the natural rate of soil erosion across the globe by a factor of ten.

But it's not all doom and gloom! In this age of increased awareness of the earth's fragility, we are seeing a strong movement toward a different way of living, one that acknowledges the central importance of conserving natural resources and biodiversity and sustaining a healthy planetary ecosystem. More and more people are embracing sustainability in every facet of their daily lives, from the clothes and household products they buy to the food they eat and the way they grow their gardens.

Though sustainability means different things to different people, in general, a sustainable garden is one that grows, thrives, looks beautiful, and supports a diverse community of flora and fauna—all without depleting the earth's natural resources. A truly sustainable garden enriches and helps restore the biosphere. Good soil care is a central component of the sustainable garden.

As much as possible, the sustainable gardener attempts to mimic nature and create a closed-loop system. Instead of using energy- and pollution-intensive inputs to enhance soil fertility, such as synthetic or mined fertilizers (or processed products from industries with questionable sustainability credentials), the sustainable gardener recycles organic waste from renewable domestic, local, or municipal sources and recruits the organisms of the soil food web to turn it into a natural soil builder. Tillage of the soil—which exposes

Soils with a loose, granular structure have ideal physical properties for supporting plant root growth and a rich system of microscopic life.

it to erosion by water and wind, destroys soil organisms, and accelerates the loss of organic matter—is minimized or replaced with more nurturing soil techniques such as mulching.

This handbook teaches you the basics of sustainable soil care. The first three chapters deal with the physical, biological, and chemical properties of soil and how they interact to determine soil health and fertility. The next chapter, "Getting to Know Your Soil," offers simple, hands-on techniques for discovering the unique characteristics of your garden soil. The following four chapters discuss the use of organic conditioners, fertilizers, and mulches in building and maintaining long-term soil fertility. "Soil Care Strategies" is a guide to resource-wise gardening. Part one, "Gardening in Challenging Conditions," tackles what are typically referred to as problem soils (for example, soils with slow drainage) and advocates the "right plant, right place" philosophy. Truly problematic soils— compacted and contaminated soils—are also addressed, along with a simple technique for overcoming soil shortfalls: gardening in raised beds. Part two gives general tips on soil care for specific plants: trees, shrubs, perennials, roses, lawn grasses, annuals, and vegetables.

At a casual glance, soil may appear pretty unremarkable—a ubiquitous amalgam of stones and other inert matter, whose one redeeming quality seems to be that it's handy for holding up plants. But dig a little deeper (figuratively speaking), and you'll find that the case is quite the opposite: Soil is a complex ecosystem, teeming with microscopic life. Moreover, the health of your soil and the creatures living in it determine your plants' health—and ultimately our own.

The Physical Properties of Soil

Stephanie Murphy

Soil is the naturally occurring mixture of weathered mineral particles and organic matter blanketing most of the earth's terrestrial surface. Though it may appear solid as you're walking on it in the garden, it's actually quite porous, and the contents of the spaces between the solids—air and water—are also considered components of the soil. The relative volume of each component varies in different soils, but good garden topsoil generally consists of around 45 percent mineral particles, 5 percent organic matter, 25 percent air, and 25 percent water. Maintaining a balance of these components is important for supporting a diverse community of beneficial fungi, bacteria, and other soil organisms and for growing healthy plants.

Components of the Soil

Weathered Rock Most soils are "mineral soils," meaning their solid portion is composed primarily of weathered rock fragments, derived either from underlying bedrock or from sediment transported and deposited from elsewhere by water, wind, or glacial ice. (In contrast, "organic soils," including peats, are very high in organic matter and form mainly in low-oxygen environments such as wetlands.) The breakdown of rock into mineral soil particles is a slow, natural process of weathering caused by physical, chemical, and biological forces. Exposure to temperature changes; abrasion by water, ice, and wind; and the expansion power of plant roots causes the physical breakdown of rocks into smaller and smaller pieces. Rock also breaks down chemically over time in the presence of rainwater and oxygen, as well as biochemically due to the release of weak organic acids by microbes, mosses, and lichens. The end products of all this weathering are the mineral ingredients of the soil—sand, silt, and clay particles and nutrient elements essential for plant growth.

Organic Matter Soil organic matter is an umbrella term encompassing the living organisms of the soil food web (see "Ecology of the Soil," page 14) and the decaying remains of dead plants, animals, and soil organisms that are part of the web. As soil organisms decompose organic matter residue, they recycle nutrients into the soil and form humus. This rich, dark substance comprises 60 to 80 percent of soil organic matter and is relatively resistant to further decay. Humus is the cornerstone of healthy soil ecosystems. Among its many benefits, humus builds and stabilizes soil structure, improves aeration, buffers excessive acidity and alkalinity in the soil, and ties up certain heavy metals. Like clay particles (see below), humus contains many small pore spaces and negative electrochemical charges, and this enables it to

The mineral components sand, silt, and clay in the right proportions and bound together with organic matter produces loam—the ideal soil for farming and gardening.

retain large amounts of water and nutrients. Replenishing and maintaining humus by using organic amendments and mulches is essential to sustainable soil care.

Air A productive soil is made up of around 50 percent pore space, containing roughly equal volumes of air and water. An adequate supply of air in the soil is a requirement for plants and most soil fauna. To get the energy they need to grow and function, plant roots must—like people and most other organisms—respire, or metabolize sugar in the presence of oxygen. A by-product of this respiration is carbon dioxide, which must be ventilated from the root zone and replaced with fresh oxygen from the atmosphere. Air diffuses in and out of the soil most rapidly through large pores, or macropores, which include earthworm tunnels and the spaces between sand particles. An abundance of macropores linking the soil to the atmosphere guarantees good air circulation for the roots of your plants. Anything severing the link—such as compaction, water (saturation), or a layer of concrete or fill—can deprive roots of oxygen.

Water A network of continuous large pores also guarantees a soil's permeability to water, essential for the survival of plants, not to mention all soil life. Plants absorb water through their roots and use it to photosynthesize sugar, transport dissolved nutrients, and much more. Macropores control how well water infiltrates the soil surface and percolates downward; however, it's the small pores—or micropores—found between particles of clay and organic matter that are primarily responsible for how well a soil retains water and stores it for later consumption by plants. Unlike macro-

pores, which drain relatively quickly due to gravitational pull on water, micropores can hold onto and conduct water against the force of gravity, moving it sideways or upward through the soil by capillary action to replenish supplies depleted by plant roots and evaporation. Some micropores are so small that the water in them is never available to plants, but in general, a balance of macro- and micropores in the soil will help ensure that your plants get adequate water and that excess moisture drains away to be replaced by air. As we'll see, the porosity of a soil depends on its texture and structure.

Though plant life will exploit even cracks in concrete, limited supplies of air and water available to roots make survival difficult.

A sand particle is visible to the eye, about equal in size to 1,000 silt or a million clay particles. An equivalent volume of smaller particles has a much greater surface area than that of sand.

Texture

A soil's texture—how coarse or fine it is and feels—is determined by the size of its mineral particles (sand, silt, and clay). Texture has a direct effect on the size and number of the pore spaces and overall surface area in the soil and is thus an important determinant of soil aeration, drainage, and water- and nutrient-holding capacity. It also affects the ease with which a soil can be cultivated, its tilth (see below).

Sand grains are the largest soil particles, ranging from 0.05 to 2 millimeters in diameter. They are visible to the naked eye—if one has 20/20 vision—and feel gritty between the fingers. Generally cubical or rounded in shape, they are typically composed of chemically inert quartz and other resilient minerals. Due to their size and shape, they create large pore spaces in the soil. Soils dominated by sand particles have lots of macropores and thus usually have good permeability. But by the same token, they are poor at holding onto water and dissolved nutrients. Their relative surface area is low, and this also translates to low water- and nutrient-holding capacity. On the plus side, sandy soils are generally loose, light, and easy to work.

Silt particles are microscopic, ranging in size from 0.002 to 0.05 millimeters. Silt feels smooth and floury to the touch. Though generally similar in shape and mineral composition to sand, silt particles create micropores in the soil and have larger relative surface area. As a result, silt is associated with somewhat better water and nutrient retention than sand, but slower drainage.

Clay particles are truly tiny—less than 0.002 millimeters in size. When moist, they are very cohesive and can be sticky to the touch. Because they're so small, their cumulative relative surface area is enormous: Consider that the surface area of the particles in a spoonful of clay can be the size of an American football field. Clay particles are flat in shape and often occur in stacks like tiny pancakes, and so the pores they create are very small and convoluted. These qualities give clay soils a tremendous capacity for retaining water and dissolved nutrients. Clay particles also differ from sand and silt in mineralogy and commonly have a net negative electrochemical charge on their surfaces, which further enhances their ability to retain water and positively charged nutrients. However,

Anchoring plants is one important job of soil. Plants in turn hold the soil in place with their root systems, preventing or reducing erosion by wind and water.

for all the same reasons, soils rich in clay tend to suffer from poor drainage and air circulation. They also tend to be heavy and difficult to cultivate.

Few soils are pure sand, silt, or clay. Most contain a mixture of all three and can be ordered into 1 of 12 textural classes based on the relative proportions of the different particles. See "The Texture Triangle," page 36. For instance, sands and loamy sands (the "light" soils) are comprised of more than 70 percent sand particles and are dominated by the properties of sand discussed above. Clays, sandy clays, and silty clays (the "heavy" soils) contain more than 40 percent clay particles and share the characteristics of clay. Loams share properties associated with all three particle types and generally make the best garden soils. They contain a balance of large and small pores and thus exhibit good air and water flow as well as moisture and nutrient retention. They are also relatively easy to cultivate. Notice that particles larger than sand (gravel, stones, rocks, etc.) are not included when quantifying soil texture; percentages of sand plus silt plus clay add up to 100. To determine your soil's texture, see "Getting to Know Your Soil," page 34.

Though loams are generally the most desirable garden soils, almost any texture of soil can be used to grow beautiful plants (see "Gardening in Challenging Conditions," page 78). Moreover, soils that are very sandy or clayey can be improved in a sustainable way by adding organic matter, which modifies another important physical property of soil— its structure.

Structure

Soil structure refers to shapes made by sand, silt, clay, and organic-matter particles when they cluster or bind together. Soil particles become grouped together into structural units called aggregates or peds by a number of different forces, including freezing and thawing, the movement and growth of plant roots, fungal activity, and the burrowing of small animals. These naturally formed peds are distinct from clods, chunks of compressed soil formed by human activities such as plowing.

Good-quality topsoil has a granular or crumb structure in which the individual peds range in size from roughly one to ten millimeters in diameter. A granular soil contains a good balance of interconnected macropores (in between peds) and micropores (within each ped). It acts like a sponge, allowing water from the soil surface to infiltrate the large pores with ease, absorbing and retaining moisture in the small pores, and allowing excess water to drain down and be replaced by air. Soils with loose, granular structure have good tilth, meaning they have ideal physical properties for supporting plant root growth and are easy to work.

Not all soils have this granular structure. Soil particles may also aggregate into large, irregular blocks, tight vertical columns, or flat horizontal plates. These structure types, which are less favorable to root growth and water or air movement, are more commonly associated with subsoil rather than topsoil but may be exposed at the surface by erosion or "mining" of the topsoil during land development. "Platy" structure, multiple layers of flat, thin peds, often results from compaction and can be found at the surface or subsurface, impeding water, air, and roots. Finally, some soils have no structure at all. They are either "single-grained" and don't cohere (a common occurrence in very sandy soils) or "massive," that is, completely consolidated into a tight, lifeless mass (as can happen in very clayey soils).

The key to creating and maintaining good crumb structure in your garden soil is organic matter. Soil organic matter provides the "glue" that binds soil particles together and the energy for the soil organisms whose activities form and stabilize granular aggregates. Applying organic amendments and mulches to your soil is the most effective and sustainable way to build and maintain good structure and, in turn, grow beautiful, healthy plants. It's also important to protect your soil's structure by reducing tillage and any other activity that fractures or crushes natural aggregates. These include digging or walking on the soil when it's wet.

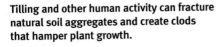
Tilling and other human activity can fracture natural soil aggregates and create clods that hamper plant growth.

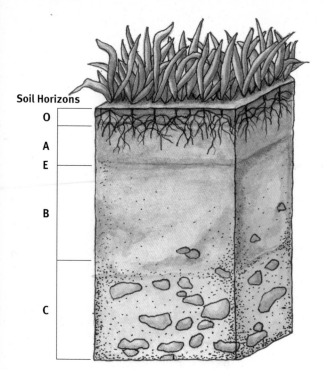

Soil Horizons

O

A
E

B

C

Layers in the Soil

Soils vary widely due to the factors influencing their formation (see next page). The variation occurs not just at the soil surface but also in the layers, or horizons, that develop from the surface down to the bedrock. Soil scientists commonly recognize six master horizons, designated by the letters O, A, E, B, C, and R, in order of depth; but it's rare that a profile will show all the horizons.

For gardeners, the most important layers are O, A, and B. The O horizon refers to the organic layer at the surface—leaf litter and other plant residue in various stages of decomposition. Below that is the A horizon, a predominantly mineral layer enriched with organic matter from the O horizon by the mixing action of soil organisms; it is distinctly darker in color than the horizons below due to the organic matter content. Commonly referred to as topsoil, this is the most fertile and biologically active zone of the soil; most plant roots are concentrated here. The B horizon roughly corresponds to the subsoil. It has less biological activity and organic matter than the A horizon but acts as an important nutrient and water reserve. Generally more tightly packed than the topsoil, it may contain higher levels of clay than topsoil, rinsed from the A horizon into the B horizon over centuries or millennia. (Most of this leaching occurs at the interface of the A and B horizons, in a zone called the E horizon.) Underneath the B horizon is the C horizon, which consists of unconsolidated material relatively unaffected by biological activity and other soil-formation processes. The final horizon is the R horizon, or underlying bedrock.

Gardeners should familiarize themselves with their topsoil and subsoil layers. Well-developed topsoil—which forms naturally under grassland and forest in humid areas—may be six to eight inches thick or more and can support a wide array of trees, shrubs, and perennials. If your topsoil is very thin, you may need to build it up by incorporating organic matter or have new soil trucked in. An ideal subsoil is permeable, allowing good drainage and deep root penetration. Subsoil that is too clayey or compacted can cause waterlogging of the topsoil, in which case you may want to modify the subsoil (a difficult job) or select plants that tolerate wet conditions.

THE FORMATION OF DIFFERENT SOILS

There is great diversity of soils across the landscape and the continent. Thousands of soil types have been named, and they are distinguished from each other by their mineral and organic content, physical characteristics, layering, and more. A number of factors combine to give the soil in each geographic region its unique qualities.

- **Parent Material** In mineral soils, "parent material" refers to the original rock or transported deposit that was weathered to "give birth" to the mineral particles of the soil. The parent material strongly influences a soil's physical and chemical properties. For instance, soils that form from a bedrock of limestone are often alkaline (see "Understanding Soil pH," page 28).

- **Climate** Climate determines the type and extent of the weathering that parent material is subjected to and the rate at which organic matter accumulates. More developed soils occur in regions with warm temperatures and abundant rainfall. Fewer plants grow in dry climates, so less organic matter builds up.

- **Living Organisms** Plants and animals affect soil development in many ways, such as by weathering rock, adding organic matter, aggregating soil particles, cycling nutrients, and mixing soil layers. Humans modify soil by activities such as gardening, agriculture, logging, and construction.

- **Relief** Topographical differences affect soil development. Soils on slopes tend to be thinner than soils on low-lying areas, due to their greater susceptibility to erosion. They also tend to be drier because of the gravitational movement of water downhill. Soils on south-facing slopes are warmer than those on north-facing slopes, and this leads to differences in weathering and biological activity.

- **Time** All soils take a long time to form naturally, which is one good reason, among many, to preserve and manage them wisely. But some soils take longer than others to mature (or develop a deep, distinct profile) due to climate and other factors. A desert soil may be chronologically old but "young" in profile—rocky, with a thin layer of topsoil and little organic matter.

Lichens contribute to soil formation by releasing weak organic acids that slowly weather rock.

Ecology of the Soil

Sina Adl

Like a rainforest or coral reef, the soil in your garden is an astonishingly complex ecosystem comprising a wide variety of interacting organisms—producers and consumers, predators and prey. These include earthworms, centipedes, and other creatures visible to the naked eye, as well as diverse populations of fungi, bacteria, and other tiny organisms only visible to us through the lens of a microscope. A gram of fresh garden topsoil (about the size of the top joint of your little finger) can contain billions of organisms, representing thousands of species (see examples on page 18). Protecting and nurturing their habitat is an important endeavour in and of itself, but it's also the key to growing healthy, beautiful plants.

Soil organisms perform a number of indispensable services for plants. These include converting atmospheric nitrogen into mineral form usable by plants (nitrogen fixation), aiding in the uptake of nutrients, aerating the soil through burrowing and other activities, breaking down toxic organic compounds such as pesticides, and suppressing outbreaks of soil-borne diseases. But probably their most important contribution is the decomposition of organic matter (dead plant and animal tissue).

Organic matter is the energy source that drives the soil ecosystem, or food web. As soil organisms break down organic matter, they recycle essential nutrients back into the soil, return carbon dioxide into the atmosphere (to be used by plants in photosynthesis), and contribute to the formation of humus, which—among its many benefits—improves the soil's capacity to retain nutrients and water. Nurture your soil organisms with annual additions of organic matter, such as good-quality compost, and they will, in turn, nurture your plants.

Soil organisms occupy many different habitat niches among the large and small pores of the soil. For example, some are adapted to live in the humid, air-filled pores themselves; others ply their trade in the thin film of water coating soil particles and aggregates. Most of them need a balanced mix of air and moisture in the soil to survive—and that's just what most garden plants need too. Medium-textured loam soils and other soils with loose, granular structure provide this balance of aeration and water retention. While it's difficult to modify the texture of your soil (how coarse or fine it is), it's relatively easy to improve its structure (the way the soil particles aggregate) by adding organic matter. (For more on soil texture and structure, see pages 9 to 11.)

Huge numbers of tiny soil organisms like this springtail participate in the breakdown of organic matter, recycling essential nutrients back into the soil and contributing to the formation of humus, which improves the soil's capacity to retain nutrients and water.

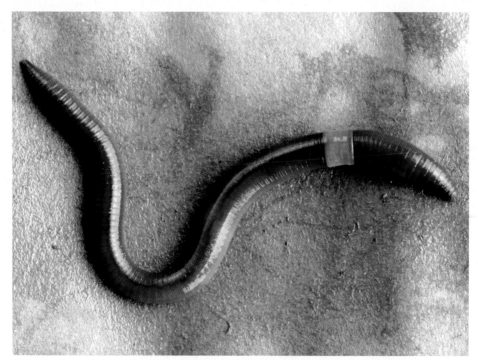
Soil macrofauna like earthworms feed on soil and decomposing matter, ingesting smaller fry along with it. Their movement through the topsoil also aerates it and incorporates organic matter.

Components of the Soil Food Web: Primary Consumers

In soil ecology, organisms are grouped together based on their roles as consumers in the soil food web. At the base of the web are the primary consumers, or decomposers (ecologists call them the primary saprotrophs), mainly fungi and bacteria, which are capable of directly digesting organic matter. They feed by secreting enzymes that break down the matter into simple organic molecules and water-soluble mineral nutrients. They then absorb a portion of the nutrients, temporarily "immobilizing" or tying them up in their cells. The nutrients are released or "mineralized" again once the fungi and bacteria die or are eaten by predators.

Fungi The organisms of this kingdom, which include molds, mildews, yeasts, mushrooms, smuts, and rusts, typically grow as thin branching filaments called hyphae. An individual fungus can spread out in the soil to cover an enormous area (the largest so far discovered extended over 1,500 acres), and some can live to be hundreds of years old. Fungi are more effective than bacteria at breaking down the complex carbon compounds of plant tissue such as cellulose or lignin, which make up the bulk of soil organic matter. Different species prefer different components of organic matter and grow at different times of the year, but all of them need oxygen to survive.

Besides decomposing organic matter and releasing nutrients, fungi help out plants in other important ways too. Several genera of fungi capture and feed on nematodes (roundworms), often ones that parasitize plant roots. More significantly, some fungi enter symbiotic associations with plant roots—called mycorrhizae—that confer enormous mutual benefit (see "Marvelous Mycorrhizae," page 20).

Bacteria These single-celled or filamentous microorganisms occur in vast numbers and diversity in the soil. Some species require oxygen, and others require an oxygen-free (anaerobic) environment. Though not as adept as fungi at decomposing plant cell walls and lignin, bacteria are nonetheless vital to the process of organic matter decomposition because they can break down organic molecules that fungi cannot. Some bacteria are also capable of breaking down human-made organic toxins, such as some herbicides and pesticides. A small number of bacteria genera also play a crucial role in how nitrogen is recycled in nature (see "The Nitrogen Cycle," page 33), fixing it from the air into the soil, transforming it from a gas into nitrogen compounds that plants can use, and—in the case of some anaerobic bacteria—converting it from mineral form back into a gas (and thus causing it to be lost from the soil ecosystem). Actinobacteria and myxobacteria, responsible for the "earthy" smell of soil, also release antibiotics that help keep other burgeoning bacterial populations in check.

Secondary Consumers

The next level of the food web is occupied by the secondary consumers, which are, unsurprisingly, the species that feed on the primary consumers. Feeders on bacteria include thousands of species of unicellular and multicellular microorganisms such as protists (for example, amoebae) and many species of nematodes. They eat bacteria and then excrete nitrogen wastes such as ammonium (absorbed directly by plants) and undigested remains, which become part of the soil organic matter and are further digested by bacteria and fungi. Fungi are eaten by specialized species of naked amoebae, testate (shell-bearing) amoebae, and nematodes, as well as many mites and collembola (springtails), all of which enrich the soil with their nitrogenous excretions and partly digested organic matter.

Higher-Level Consumers

Secondary consumers are, in turn, eaten by higher-level consumers. There are predatory mites that capture and eat nematodes, other mites, and collembola; nematodes that ingest protists; and species of protists that prey on other protists. Again, the fecal pellets of these species become part of the soil organic matter, fed upon by fungi and bacteria; and their nitrogenous wastes increase the fertility of the soil.

Earthworms Larger animals such as earthworms and many insect larvae eat mouthfuls of soil and decomposing organic matter. They feed directly on the decomposing organic matter (making them primary consumers) but also on the species ingested along with the soil. Burrowing earthworms also play an important

Key Players in the Soil Food Web

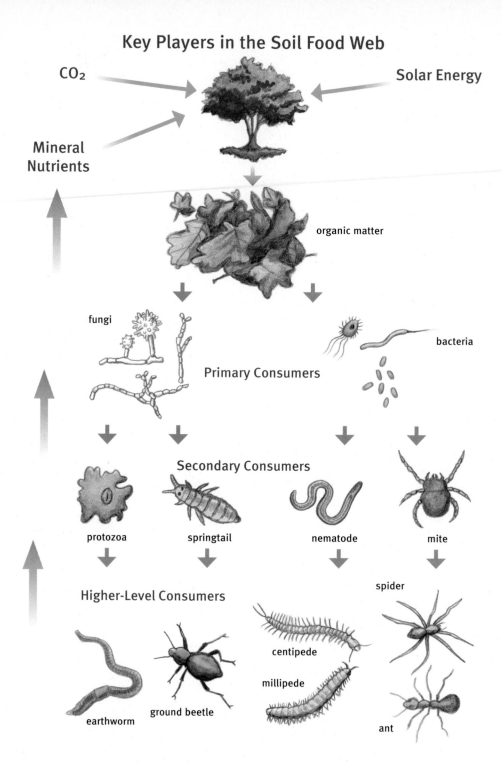

CO₂

Solar Energy

Mineral Nutrients

organic matter

fungi

bacteria

Primary Consumers

Secondary Consumers

protozoa   springtail   nematode   mite

spider

Higher-Level Consumers

centipede

millipede

earthworm   ground beetle   ant

Organisms are grouped together based on their roles as consumers in the soil food web. Arrows indicate how energy is transferred through the levels of the web. (Not to scale.)

Moles may not have many fans among gardeners, but their presence does indicate healthy populations of insects and earthworms in the soil.

role in many ecosystems, in particular the garden, by aerating the soil and dragging organic matter from the surface down into the root zone.

Surface Predators Many animal species occupy the soil surface, especially if there is leaf-litter cover. These include arthropods such as centipedes, millipedes, ants, ground beetles, and spiders. Some are predatory, while others shred and eat decomposing debris. They can all become food for larger surface dwellers like birds and rodents. The presence of spiders, ground beetles, and other predators is a good indicator of a healthy soil, because it shows that sufficient numbers of prey organisms are at work.

How Soil Organisms Interact with Plant Roots

Plant roots aren't just passive "observers" of all this food-web activity in the soil. The highest levels of microbial diversity and other animal life occur in the rhizosphere—the zone of soil extending roughly two millimeters out from plant roots. And there's a good reason for it. Plants actively secrete sugars and amino acids from pioneer cells, specialized cells at the tips of new roots. These root exudates promote the growth of bacteria and fungi, concentrating microbial decomposition and nutrient release where it's needed the most. Pioneer cells also secrete substances that temporarily inactivate nematodes, thus protecting the root tips from parasitic infections.

MARVELOUS MYCORRHIZAE

Some fungi form close, symbiotic associations with the roots of plants. Known as mycorrhizae, these mutually beneficial associations allow for the exchange of water and nutrients between fungal and plant cells. The fungus receives sugars and amino acids from the plant, while the plant receives phosphates and other essential nutrients from the fungus. Water uptake by the plant may also be enhanced by mycorrhizae.

Mycorrhizal fungi form networks of very fine strands that can extend many yards from the colonized plant root into the surrounding soil, significantly increasing the absorptive surface of the plant root system. In addition, due to their diminutive size, fungal hyphae can mine nutrients from clays and obtain water from small soil pores much more effectively than root hairs. Experiments have shown that mycorrhizae enhance plant growth and make plants more resilient to drought stress. There is also evidence that mycorrhizae protect plant roots from certain fungal pathogens by competing with the pathogens for entry sites.

Most plant species, including the majority of crops and garden ornamentals, form associations with mycorrhizal fungi. Two general types of mycorrhizae are recognized. Ectomycorrhizae are mainly associated with certain temperate-climate and semiarid-climate trees (including conifers, beeches, birches, oaks, poplars, and willows). Though some of their hyphae penetrate the plant roots by passing between cell walls, most of them form sheaths around the surfaces of root tips to facilitate nutrient exchange. Endomycorrhizae (pictured here) are much more common, occurring with most other plants; their hyphae penetrate the cell walls (but not the cell membranes) of plant roots, branching profusely inside the plant cell to increase the surface area for nutrient exchange.

In normal, biologically active soil, sufficient mycorrhizal fungi are usually present to establish robust associations with plants. However, in highly disturbed or infertile soils, native populations of mycorrhizal fungi are often low or absent. In such situations, the use of mycorrhizal inoculants can lead to dramatic increases in plant survival and growth. Commercial ectomycorrhizae are widely available because they're relatively easy to culture. Endo-mycorrhizal inoculation is usually carried out by bringing in soil from nearby healthy ecosystems that contain matching plant species.

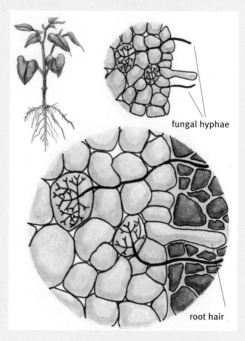

fungal hyphae

root hair

Food Web Contributions to Soil Structure

The organisms in soil build structure by providing organic matter—in the form of decomposing plant and animal tissue as well as fecal pellets produced by the organisms. They also create and stabilize structure in other ways. For instance, bacteria produce a slimy, sticky coating around themselves called a capsule. This substance helps attach them to soil particles so they aren't readily washed away by rain. The large numbers of bacteria present in the soil help stick soil particles together, thus enhancing structure. Fungal hyphae grow and form an extensive mesh that also holds soil particles together—improving structure in much the same way that plant roots do. Proteins secreted by the fungi and bacteria into the soil also contribute to the collection of particles into loose, granular aggregates called peds (see "Structure," page 10).

Suppression of Soil Pathogens and Pests

As any gardener who has struggled with diseases such as wilt, canker, and leaf spot knows, not all soil organisms are beneficial to plants. However, in a healthy soil supporting a complete food web, there is usually sufficient diversity to keep disease-causing species in check. That is not to say the soil will be disease free, but rather that the impacts of disease organisms will be dramatically reduced.

Most plant pathogens happen to be fungi, and they tend to spend at least part of their life cycle in the soil. For example, germination of fungal spores often takes place in the soil environment. If there are sufficient active fungal-feeding species present, many of these spores will be eaten before they begin to grow and spread.

The food web also contains animal species that parasitize plant roots, such as some types of nematodes. Other animal parasites include mites that hatch in the soil and as juveniles climb onto plants to feed. Many insect pests also begin their life as eggs or larvae in the soil. If sufficient predatory species are present in the soil or on the surface, a large portion of the insect pests' eggs and larvae will be eaten before they have a chance to cause harm. Predators include some mites, spiders, and centipedes and also many insects and insect larvae.

Caring for the Life in Your Soil

The bottom line: Create a healthy soil environment and nurture a biodiverse soil food web, and in addition to improving fertility and tilth, you should be less troubled by soil-borne plant diseases and pests. Following are tips on how to foster the food web in your garden.

Provide a well-aerated and evenly moist soil. Poor drainage restricts airflow and makes soil prone to anaerobic conditions, which encourage denitrifying bacteria and thus the loss of valuable nitrogen from the soil to the air. Wet, poorly aerated conditions also promote fungal root diseases.

The Smallest Soil Builders
Typical number of microorganisms in a gram of topsoil

Organism (dry weight)

Bacteria: 10 million to 10 billion

Fungi: 1,000 to 100,000 meters per gram

Protozoa: 1 million to 100 million

Nematodes: 10 to 100

Mites and collembola: 10 to 1,000

Nematodes and countless other tiny soil dwellers enrich the soil with their nitrogenous excretions.

Provide a regular supplement of organic matter, such as compost and mulch. This provides food for your soil web creatures but also enhances the environment in which they live. Moreover, good-quality mature compost acts as an inoculant, adding diverse populations of beneficial organisms to your soil.

Balance the carbon and nitrogen ratio of your compost ingredients. This will encourage a healthy mix of fungi and bacteria and associated feeders. (See "Compost: Homemade Humus for Healthy Soils," page 50.)

Keep the soil pH close to neutral. Strongly acidic or alkaline conditions reduce microbial activity (and thus nutrient cycling) in the soil. The most diverse populations of fungi and bacteria are present in soils with pH close to neutral.

Avoid activities that cause compaction. For starters, don't work the soil when it's wet. Compaction collapses the pore spaces in which soil organisms live and breathe and prevents the healthy growth of plant roots. (See "Compacted Soils," page 92.)

Avoid or minimize tillage of soil. It disrupts the food web and destroys soil structure. Fungal hyphae, in particular, are easily broken up by soil disturbance.

Respond to pest or disease outbreaks. Use the most effective, least-toxic controls possible in order to protect the beneficial organisms in your soil. Purchase beneficial insects and nematodes to control aboveground or belowground pests, rotate vegetable crops and annuals, choose disease-resistant plants, and promptly remove diseased plant material from the garden. See the Brooklyn Botanic Garden handbooks *Natural Insect Control* and *Natural Disease Control* for details.

CUSTOMIZING THE SOIL FOOD WEB

Organic gardeners have long known the benefits of nurturing the soil food web through such practices as applying regular doses of good-quality organic matter. In recent years, however, some landscape specialists have been working to refine organic soil-care methods based on the discovery in the 1980s that the ratio of fungi to bacteria varies in different soils.

In general, fungi tend to dominate the active microbial biomass in undisturbed environments—especially forests—because they are more efficient decomposers of organic matter than bacteria. The biomass of bacteria tends to be higher than that of fungi in other soils, such as those associated with prairies and rangeland. In addition, because fungal hyphae are easily destroyed by disturbance—such as plowing—they are generally less prevalent in agricultural soils.

From these general observations, some organic-gardening practitioners have concluded that plants adapted to different habitats are also adapted to different fungal-bacterial ratios—in short, that trees, shrubs, and perennials prefer fungus-dominated soils and that grasses, annuals, and vegetable crops prefer bacteria-dominated soils.

Some go further and say—controversially—that gardeners should customize their composts and mulches to promote fungal or bacterial dominance, depending on the plants they're growing. For instance, brown mulches, such as bark and wood chips, are recommended to promote fungal growth, and green mulches, such as grass clippings, are recommended to increase the bacterial biomass. Customized microbial teas are also recommended as a management tool for restoring fungi and bacteria to soils in the appropriate ratios (see "Compost Tea," page 57).

So far, there is no published evidence to support claims that particular crops prefer a particular ratio of fungus to bacteria. Moreover, by itself, the biomass ratio doesn't tell us anything about whether the correct combination of fungal and bacteria species is present—and active—to carry out efficient decomposition. Current research in soil microbiology is focused not on ratios but on the diversity and activity of fungi and bacteria, and DNA analysis is being used to explore and understand how different combinations of microbes work together.

Mulching is sound gardening practice. Whether it's worthwhile customizing mulches to promote fungal or bacterial dominance in the soil is under investigation.

Soil Fertility and the Essential Nutrients

Niall Dunne

In the animal kingdom, you are what you eat; in the plant kingdom, however, you are what you absorb. About 90 percent of a plant's living tissue is water, which is absorbed from the soil by the plant roots. Much of the rest of the plant (living and nonliving matter) consists of carbon, oxygen, and hydrogen. The carbon derives from atmospheric carbon dioxide that diffuses into the plant through leaf pores called stomata; the hydrogen and oxygen come from soil water that's transported to the leaves and combined with carbon dioxide during photosynthesis to produce sugars.

Carbon, oxygen, and hydrogen are clearly vital to your vegetation; but plants must absorb 13 other elements—the essential nutrients—in order to complete their life cycles. These range from familiar elements such as nitrogen to lesser-known ones such as molybdenum. Each performs at least one important, non-substitutable task. Nitrogen, for example, forms a major part of all proteins, including the enzymes that control virtually every biological process in plants. Molybdenum is a component of just one particular enzyme, nitrate reductase, which enables plants to assimilate nitrogen into their cells.

Plants get their nutrients from the soil. They absorb them at the roots in the form of mineral ions—electrically charged atoms or molecules—dissolved in soil water. These are either cations (positively charged ions) such as ammonium (NH_4^+), potassium (K^+), and calcium (Ca^{2+}), or anions (negatively charged ions) such as nitrate (NO_3^-), phosphate (PO_4^{3-}), and sulfate (SO_4^{2-}). As roots absorb these nutrients, they actively pump out hydrogen ions (H^+) and hydroxide ions (OH^-) to maintain electrochemical balance in the plant tissue and stimulate further nutrient exchange with the soil.

Key Factors Affecting Nutrient Availability

At any one time, the bulk of the nutrient pool in the soil is tied up in insoluble form in soil minerals or organic matter. It becomes available in soluble ionic form via weathering of mineral matter and decomposition of organic matter. The rate of nutrient release from physical and chemical weathering of rock is slow and depends upon numerous factors, especially climate. The rate at which organic matter releases nutrients is much faster and is determined by the diversity and activity of organisms in your soil. That's why replenishing organic matter and nurturing a healthy soil food web are important for the long-term fertility of your soil (see "Ecology of the Soil," page 14).

This stand of corn is growing on a hillside where water collects at the bottom. Organic matter decomposition is slower in wet soil due to low levels of oxygen, so nutrients like nitrogen are less available to the plants, which shows in the discolored foliage.

The availability of essential nutrients to plants is strongly influenced by soil pH—the measure of acidity or alkalinity (see "Understanding Soil pH," page 28). The majority of nutrients are able to form soluble ions or compounds when the soil pH is in the slightly acidic range of 6 to 6.8. Not surprisingly, most plants are happiest in this pH range. Extreme acidity and alkalinity restrict certain nutrients from entering the soil solution and can release other nutrients and minerals in toxic amounts.

Cation Exchange

Cation exchange capacity (CEC)—a soil's ability to hold onto cation nutrients in the face of leaching by rain and irrigation water—is another important determinant of nutrient availability, and thus fertility. Clay particles and organic matter have negative charges on their surfaces and thus are able to attract and retain cations, which can eventually be exchanged for H^+ with plant roots. Soils that are rich in clay and organic matter have high CEC, whereas soils composed mainly of sand particles (which are chemically inert) have low CEC. Adding organic matter such as compost to your soil is the most effective way to increase CEC and nutrient retention.

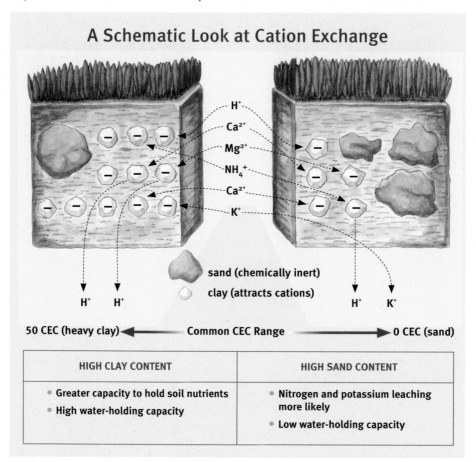

A Schematic Look at Cation Exchange

H^+
Ca^{2+}
Mg^{2+}
NH_4^+
Ca^{2+}
K^+

sand (chemically inert)
clay (attracts cations)

H^+ H^+

H^+ K^+

50 CEC (heavy clay) ◀——— Common CEC Range ———▶ 0 CEC (sand)

HIGH CLAY CONTENT	HIGH SAND CONTENT
• Greater capacity to hold soil nutrients • High water-holding capacity	• Nitrogen and potassium leaching more likely • Low water-holding capacity

Nutrient Deficiencies and Imbalances

An ideal soil contains sufficient quantities of all the essential plant minerals. However, fertility varies from place to place due to factors such as parent material, climate, and land-use history, and it's not uncommon for soils to be limited in one or more nutrients. Indeed, the primary macronutrients—nitrogen, phosphorus, and potassium—are often in low supply in most soils because, among other reasons, they are the minerals most in demand by plants. Moreover, nitrogen in its anion form—nitrate (NO_3^-)—is quickly lost from the soil because, unlike a cation, it is repelled by the negative charges on the surfaces of organic matter and clay and leaches readily.

Some nutrient imbalances offer visual cues, such as this infestation of aphids, which may indicate an overabundance of nitrogen in the soil.

Along with sufficient quantities of each nutrient, a soil must also contain them in balanced supply. High concentrations of essential minerals can cause developmental problems in plants and be toxic to soil microbes. For example, excess nitrogen can overstimulate leaf growth at the expense of flower formation and make plant foliage more susceptible to pests; too much sulfur can cause premature dropping of leaves. Also, excessive amounts of one nutrient can tie up another: Too much copper in the soil, for instance, causes molybdenum deficiency; excess potassium causes shortages of boron.

The physical condition of your plants can provide an indication of nutrient problems in the soil. Plants deficient in phosphorus, for example, typically develop purple shading on their leaves and stems. However, visual cues can also cause confusion because a number of the nutrient deficiency symptoms overlap (it's hard to tease apart sulfur from nitrogen deficiency, for instance). In addition, the symptoms of attack by certain diseases and pests resemble the symptoms of some nutrient deficiencies.

Getting your soil formally tested is the most accurate way to estimate its nutrient status (see "Getting to Know Your Soil," page 34) and make informed and sustainable decisions about what, if anything, needs to be done to improve fertility. An overview of the essential nutrients and symptoms of deficiencies begins on page 30.

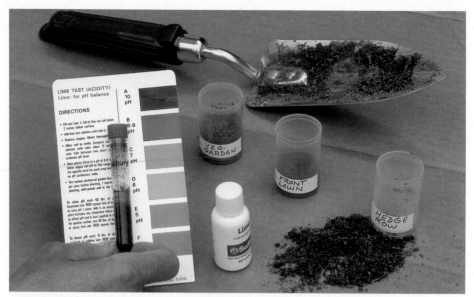

A home pH kit may be helpful in giving you a general idea of your soil's pH. The most accurate way to determine pH is to have the soil checked by a soil-test lab.

Understanding Soil pH

A soil's pH is a measure of its acidity or alkalinity—or more precisely, the acidity or alkalinity of the water held in its pores. The acidity or alkalinity of soil water (or any solution) is determined by the relative concentration of hydrogen ions (H^+) to hydroxyl ions (OH^-) present. If the H^+ ions predominate, then the soil is acidic; if the OH^- ions are more concentrated, then the soil is alkaline. If the ions balance each other out (as they do in pure water), then the soil is neutral.

The pH scale is based on the activity of the H^+ ions (the letters *pH* stand for "potential hydrogen" or "power of hydrogen"). It runs from 1 to 14, with 1 representing extreme acidity, 14 representing extreme alkalinity, and 7 representing neutral. It's an inverse scale: As the pH numbers decrease, the concentration of H^+ ions (and thus the acidity) increases. It's also a logarithmic scale, such that each unit change represents a tenfold difference in alkalinity or acidity. For example, a solution with a pH of 3 (vinegar, say) is ten times more acidic than a solution with a pH of 4 (beer).

So why are all these technical details important to gardeners? The pH of your soil has a significant effect on the availability of different plant nutrients (see the graph on the facing page). In strongly acidic soils (pH 4 to 5.5), the nutrients phosphorus, potassium, calcium, magnesium, and molybdenum are in limited supply. In medium to strongly alkaline soils (pH 8 to 10), the availability of phosphorus, iron, copper, zinc, and manganese is significantly reduced.

Furthermore, strongly acidic or alkaline conditions increase the solubility of some nutrients and other minerals, sometimes to toxic levels. For instance, in very acidic soils, iron and manganese can become so concentrated that they interfere with plant growth. An abundance of one nutrient can also reduce the solubility of another. In very alkaline soils, for example, high levels of calcium and magnesium restrain the availability of phosphorus.

Soils vary in pH depending on parent material, levels of precipitation, and human influences (see "Acidic Soils," page 78, and "Alkaline Soils," page 80). Likewise, plants vary in tolerance of acidic and alkaline conditions, based on the natural habitats to which they're adapted. However, the majority of plants prefer a pH ranging from 6 to 7—which is the range in which all the plant nutrients are most readily available. It also happens to be roughly the pH range in which soil microbes are at their most diverse and active. In very acidic or alkaline soils, nutrient cycling is slower due to the reduced numbers and activity of beneficial bacteria and fungi.

The most accurate way to determine the pH of your soil is to have it professionally tested (home test kits, available at your local garden center, are good for providing a rough estimate). If your test reveals high acidity or alkalinity, you can adjust the pH of your soil to the optimal range using a variety of amendments. Another—and more sustainable option—is to select plants that are adapted to grow in extreme pH conditions. See "Gardening in Challenging Conditions," page 78.

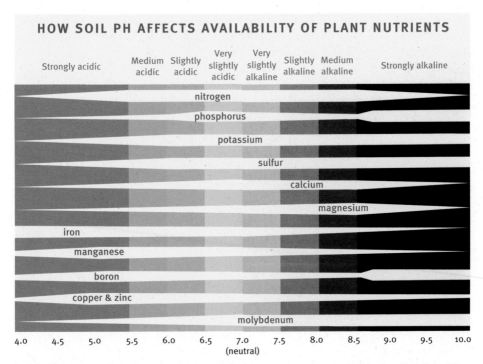

HOW SOIL PH AFFECTS AVAILABILITY OF PLANT NUTRIENTS

In general, nutrients are best available in the amounts that plants need in the slightly acidic to neutral range. In strongly acidic or alkaline soils, some nutrients may not be available to plants, and others may reach toxic levels.

The Essential Minerals

The elements essential to plants are classified as either macronutrients or micronutrients, according to their relative concentrations in plant tissue. The macronutrient nitrogen is the element plants need in the highest quantity; the micronutrient molybdenum is at the far end of the scale—plants use about a million times less of it than nitrogen. Nevertheless, both elements are essential to the health of your plants.

PRIMARY MACRONUTRIENTS

Nitrogen (N)

An essential component of nucleic acids (for example, DNA), proteins, and chlorophyll (the pigment responsible for photosynthesis), nitrogen stimulates root growth and development in plants and the uptake of other nutrients. It also encourages lush foliage growth. Unlike other mineral nutrients (which all come from rock), soil nitrogen derives almost solely from biological processes such as decomposition of organic matter and nitrogen fixation by bacteria (see "The Nitrogen Cycle," page 33). Plants absorb nitrogen in the form of nitrate (NO_3^-) and ammonium (NH_4^+). Due to its mobility in the soil, nitrate is generally more available to plants; but for the same reason, it also leaches away quickly.

Deficiency Nitrogen deficiency is common in many soils because of leaching and other factors. Plants with insufficient nitrogen develop chlorosis (yellowing of foliage), starting with the older (lower) leaves first. Growth may be stunted, and stems may become thin and spindly. However, some of these symptoms can be confused with those of *Phytophthora* root rot or *Verticillium* wilt (yellow leaves) or nematode infestation (stunting).

Renewable Sources Use compost and manure to maintain nitrogen levels in fertile soils. Use alfalfa meal, blood meal, or nitrogen-fixing legumes (see "Green Manure," page 66) in deficient soils.

Yellowing, or chlorotic, foliage is often a symptom of nitrogen deficiency.

These grape leaves look as if they were scorched by the sun, which indicates a deficiency in potassium, a primary macronutrient.

Phosphorus (P)

This mineral is another essential constituent of nucleic acids and is critical to energy storage and transfer, cell division, and early root growth in plants. Phosphorus also contributes to healthy flower, fruit, and seed formation. Plants absorb it in the form of the phosphate ion (PO_4^{3-}); the main source comes from the decomposition of organic matter.

Deficiency The supply of phosphorus is low in most soils, mainly because of the poor solubility of soil phosphates. Deficiencies are common in strongly acidic or alkaline soils and soils with high levels of aluminum. Symptoms include interrupted or delayed flowering and fruit set, stunted roots, and a purplish cast on stems and leaves.

Renewable Sources Add manure or liquid seaweed to deficient soils.

Potassium (K)

Plants need potassium for ion balance, enzyme activation, carbohydrate metabolism, and photosynthesis. It also regulates uptake of nitrogen, sodium, and calcium and helps plants develop strong root systems and disease resistance. Plants absorb it in the form of the potassium ion (K^+). The main source of potassium in the soil is slow weathering of potassium-rich minerals such as micas and feldspars and, less significantly, decomposition of organic matter.

Deficiency Potassium ions easily leach from acidic soils or soils with low CEC. Deficiency is also found in soils with excess calcium or magnesium. Symptoms include stunting, irregular yellow leaf splotches (on older leaves first), and scorched-looking leaf margins.

Renewable Sources Use compost for fertile soils; apply kelp meal or composted wood ash (for acidic soils only) in deficient soils.

SECONDARY MACRONUTRIENTS
Calcium (Ca)
This mineral has a number of functions in plants, including cell-wall development, cell division and elongation, nitrate uptake and metabolism, and protein synthesis.

Deficiency Calcium is present in adequate amounts in most soils. Deficiency is usually associated with high acidity or excess potassium. Drought can also lead to problems with calcium uptake. Symptoms include deformity of new (upper) leaves, curling and yellowing of leaf edges, stubby brown roots, and hardening of stems. Insufficient calcium causes blossom-end rot in tomatoes, peppers, and eggplant and tip burn in cabbage.

Renewable Sources Add kelp meal, bonemeal, and wood ash (acidic soils only).

Nonrenewable Sources Apply limestone to acidic soils and gypsum to alkaline soils.

Magnesium (Mg)
Magnesium forms part of the chlorophyll molecule and is thus essential for plant photosynthesis. It is also involved in enzyme activation. Plants absorb it in the form of the magnesium ion (Mg^{2+}).

Deficiency Low magnesium is usually associated with acidic, sandy soils or with excess potassium or calcium. Symptoms of deficiency include yellowing of older leaves, especially between leaf veins; thin, curling foliage; and brown spotting on leaf stalks.

Renewable Sources Coffee grounds, composted leaves, and manure can correct moderate but not high deficiency.

Nonrenewable Sources Apply dolomitic limestone to acidic soils and Epsom salts to alkaline soils.

Sulfur (S)
This macronutrient is an important component of proteins, fats, and some defensive compounds in plants. Roots absorb it in the form of sulfate (SO_4^{2-}).

Deficiency Sulfur is rarely deficient, except in soils with inadequate organic matter. Symptoms include yellowing of leaves (upper ones first); plants will be spindly and small.

Renewable Sources Compost provides the missing organic matter.

MICRONUTRIENTS
Also known as the trace minerals, the essential micronutrients are chlorine, boron, iron, manganese, zinc, copper, and molybdenum. They are needed by plants in small amounts to form complex organic molecules such as enzymes, growth hormones, proteins, and pigments (including the all-important chlorophyll). Micronutrient deficiencies are generally not common, except in very alkaline or acidic soils. To ensure a balanced supply, keep your soil's pH around neutral and maintain appropriate levels of organic matter. A balance of micronutrients is important, because any one of them in excess can be toxic to your plants and the soil community. It's not recommended to add individual micronutrients in the form of chelated fertilizers to your soil.

A lack of calcium causes blossom-end rot in tomatoes and several other garden fruits.

THE NITROGEN CYCLE

CRAIG COGGER

Managing nitrogen is a key part of growing a productive and environmentally friendly garden. It is the nutrient needed in the largest amount by plants, but excess amounts can harm plants and degrade water quality.

Most nitrogen in soil is initially tied up in organic matter in forms such as humus and proteins. This organic nitrogen, though protected from leaching, is not available to plants. As soil warms in spring, microbes begin breaking down organic matter, releasing some nitrogen as ammonium (NH_4^+), a soluble inorganic ion that plants can access. When the soil is warm, a group of microbes called nitrifiers convert the ammonium to nitrate (NO_3^-), also soluble and available to plants.

Legumes such as these sweet peas convert atmospheric nitrogen from the soil air to nitrogen available for root uptake.

Because nitrate has a negative charge, it is not held to the surface of clay or organic matter, so it can be readily lost by leaching. Nitrate remaining in the soil at the end of the growing season will leach during the fallow season in humid and subhumid climates and may reach groundwater, where it becomes a contaminant. In soils that are saturated during the wet season, anaerobic soil microbes called denitrifiers convert nitrate to nitrogen gases, which diffuse back into the atmosphere.

Ammonium and nitrate taken up by plants are converted back to organic forms in plant tissue. When plant residues are returned to the soil, they decompose, slowly releasing nitrogen back into available forms. The nitrogen cycle is a leaky one, with losses to leaching and to the atmosphere. Harvesting crops also removes nitrogen from the system. To maintain an adequate nitrogen supply, nitrogen must be added back into the system through fertilization or fixation.

Nitrogen fixation is a natural process carried out in the soil either by free-living bacteria such as *Azotobacter* or symbiotic bacteria such as *Rhizobia* and *Frankia*. The symbiotic bacteria form nodules in the roots of certain plants, and through these nodules they are able to take atmospheric nitrogen from the soil air and convert it to available nitrogen within the plant. The plants supply the bacteria with energy and nutrients. Legumes such as beans, alfalfa, and clover fix nitrogen using *Rhizobia*; alder trees fix nitrogen with *Frankia*. Growing legumes as a cover crop will supply nitrogen to future crops.

Getting to Know Your Soil

Ulrich Lorimer

Knowing the physical, chemical, and biological characteristics of your soil is vital to growing healthy plants and making informed, sustainable decisions about how to care for your garden. It's quite easy to get acquainted with the physical traits of your soil using a shovel, some elbow grease, and a few simple experiments. However, nutrient levels, pH, cation exchange capacity, and the diversity of your soil food web are best determined with the help of laboratory professionals.

Physical Characteristics

Testing Texture As described earlier, soils are categorized into textural classes (silty clay, sandy loam, and so on), based on the proportions of sand, silt, and clay present. The easiest experiment for determining the texture of your soil is the feel test. Simply scoop up some moist soil and rub it between your fingers. If it feels coarse and gritty, it's most likely predominated by sand particles; if it feels smooth and floury, your soil has a lot of silt particles; if the soil feels sticky and you can easily form a ribbon, then it has a lot of clay particles.

Another way to measure texture is by the jar test. Add two cups of garden soil to an empty quart-size jar, making sure to first remove any stones or debris from the sample. Then add a teaspoon of liquid detergent, fill the jar to the top with water, and tightly fasten the lid. Mix the solution by tipping the jar upside down and back upright for about a minute. Place the jar in a place where it won't be disturbed, and let the soil particles settle out. After about 24 hours, three relatively distinct layers of solid material should be visible in the jar. The larger, heavier sand particles will have settled out first, forming the bottommost layer. The middle layer will be composed of medium-grained silt particles, and the topmost layer will be finely textured clay. Measure the thickness of each layer with a ruler. To determine the percentages of sand, silt, and clay, simply divide the thickness of each layer in inches by the total thickness of the soil sample and multiply your answer by 100. Use the texture triangle on the next page to gauge the textural class of your soil sample.

Medium-textured soils such as sandy loam and loam have a well-balanced mix of sand, silt, and clay and (when humus content is sufficient) are generally well aerated and good at retaining moisture and nutrients. Challenges arise when the percentages of sand or clay particles are disproportionately high. As discussed in "Gardening in Challenging Conditions," page 78, sustainable solutions for sandy or clay soils include growing adapted plant species and modifying soil structure with organic matter.

Familiarize yourself with soil: Smell it, rub it between your fingers to explore texture and structure.

THE TEXTURE TRIANGLE

Scientists categorize soils into 12 textural classes based on the proportions of sand, silt, and clay present. The texture triangle below shows the mineral makeup of each of these classes and provides a useful tool for describing the texture of your own soil.

Step 1 Use the jar test described on page 35 to calculate the percentages of sand, clay, and silt in your soil sample.

Step 2 Locate the clay percentage of your soil on the left side of the triangle and follow the purple line across.

Step 3 Locate the sand percentage along the base of the triangle and follow the blue line up to where it intersects with the purple line you selected. The green line at this intersection represents the percentage of silt in your soil sample.

The shaded area that contains the point you have located describes your sample's textural class.

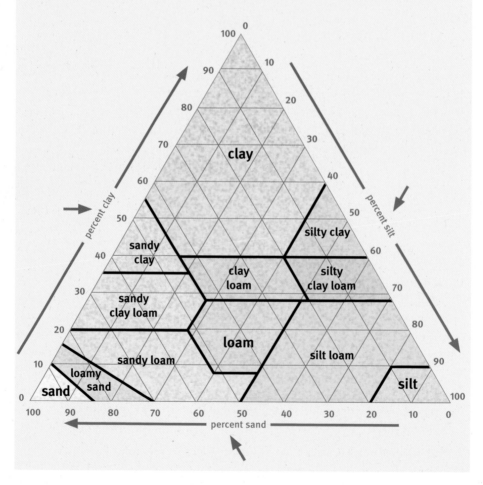

Examining Structure Soils with good structure—in which the individual soil particles group together into loose, granular aggregates—have lots of interconnecting pore spaces of varying sizes. This porous quality helps them to retain moisture and dissolved nutrients. At the same time, it makes them more permeable to water, air, and plant roots—and easier to dig and work. Good structure is present in soils with thriving communities of soil organisms and sufficient organic matter. Even heavy clay soils with good structure are quite porous and workable. One way to test the structure of your soil is to dig a hole about a foot deep and examine the size of the soil aggregates at different depths. (Of course, after digging this much into your soil, you'll automatically have a sense of how "workable" it is.)

Use a percolation test to determine drainage: Dig a hole that's a foot deep and wide, add water, and observe how long it takes for the water to disappear.

Topsoil with good structure is composed mainly of soft, rounded aggregates between about one and ten millimeters in diameter. Any large clumps should crumble under gentle pressure in your hands to form these aggregates. Heavy, clayey soils with poor structure will resist crumbling and form tight, cloddy "sausages" when rolled between both palms; light, sandy soils with poor structure won't retain any shape when squeezed. As discussed in "Conditioning Your Soil," page 42, the key to improving and maintaining good structure is adding organic matter, minimizing cultivation of the soil as much as possible, and refraining from working in the garden when soil is either too wet or too dry.

Determining Drainage Most garden plants do best in soils that retain moisture but also drain off excess water relatively quickly. To determine the drainage of your soil, you can use a straightforward percolation test. Dig a hole in your garden, about one foot wide by one foot deep. Fill the hole up to the top with water and observe what happens. If the water seeps away within a few minutes to an hour, your soil is fast draining, and you should either grow plants that thrive in dry conditions or add organic matter to improve water retention (see "Sandy Soils," page 84). If the water drains within a few hours, you have good, or "average," drainage and thus the potential to grow a wide range of plants. If there is still water in the hole after 24 hours,

From left to right: Clayey soil, loam, and sandy soil. The color provides clues about a soil's physical characteristics and fertility. Black or brown topsoil is usually rich in organic matter.

your soil is either naturally wet, possibly because of a high water table or clay content, or poorly draining, perhaps due to compaction or poor structure. (See "Wet Soils," page 86, and "Compacted Soils," page 92, for tips on gardening in these challenging conditions.)

Decoding Soil Color Soils vary in color because of differences in parent material, drainage conditions, and humus content. The color of your soil can provide important clues about its fertility and physical characteristics. Black and brown topsoils are generally rich in organic matter. Light or pale colors often indicate low organic-matter content, coarse texture, and potential for nutrient leaching. Subsoil colors can tell you a lot about how well or poorly your soil drains. Red and brown subsoils usually have good air and water movement; yellows, grays, or mottling in the subsoil usually indicate poor aeration or drainage.

Soil Chemistry: Nutrient Levels and pH

The Soil Test The most accurate way to determine the nutrient content, pH, cation exchange capacity, and salinity of your soil is to have it analyzed by a soil-testing laboratory, either a private one or a university extension lab. Most commercial labs will also analyze your soil's texture, organic-matter content, and contaminant levels for an extra fee. It's a good idea to use a lab relatively close to home, because its specialists will be more knowledgeable about your local soil conditions. To find a lab near you, contact your county's Cooperative Extension service for a referral or search online. (Check bbg.org/soils for a list of resources).

Most labs will send you a soil-test kit, with sampling instructions, a sample bag, and a survey form. Answer the questions on the form in detail so that the lab analysts can make the most informed recommendations for your garden. You can usually either mail the sample to the lab or deliver it in person. The cost of a standard test typically ranges between $25 and $40, and you usually get the results within a matter of weeks.

The test results will tell you about the chemical properties of your garden soil, what nutrients (if any) are deficient, and how to address those deficiencies. From the test results you can also determine which plants are best suited to the growing conditions in your garden. (See "Soil Care Strategies," page 76.) Following the lab's recommendations for amendments will help you avoid creating nutrient imbalances in the soil or contaminating the environment through excessive application of fertilizer. More and more university labs are providing recommendations for natural fertilizers as well as synthetics. On its website, the National Sustainable Agriculture Information Service (attra.org; 800-346-9140) features a list of private soil labs catering to organic and sustainable growers. It's generally advisable to have your soil tested every few years or so. If you are a vegetable gardener, have your soil tested more frequently to avoid unnecessary use of fertilizer (synthetic or organic).

To get the most accurate results, collect separate samples from the different planting areas in your garden. To collect a soil sample from your lawn, dig down four inches.

Taking a Sample For your test results to be accurate, your sample must be collected and handled correctly, so follow the lab instructions carefully. In general, you can sample your soil anytime the ground is not frozen. Use a hand trowel, shovel, or spade to dig up individual samples, making sure to clean tools beforehand to avoid contamination. Clear away any mulch or thatch on the ground before digging. Individual samples should be intact slabs of soil about two inches wide, one inch thick, and collected at a depth of four inches to a foot—depending on what you're planning to grow (for lawn, dig down four inches; for annuals, perennials, and vegetables, sample the first six inches; for shrubs and trees, dig down about a foot).

Sample the top six inches of soil in an area where you want to grow vegetables. You may also want to have the soil tested for contaminants like heavy metals.

Soil characteristics vary from one location in the garden to another, depending on drainage patterns and history of use. Ideally, you should collect separate samples from all the different planting areas in your garden—front lawn, back lawn, planting beds, and vegetable garden—and send them to the lab to be analyzed individually. To get a representative sample of the soil throughout the garden, dig up ten individual samples from randomly chosen locations within the garden area, mix them together in a bucket, and then spread the soil onto some newspaper to air dry. Take about a pint of dried soil, seal it in the sample bag, box the bag, and send it to the lab.

Soil Biology: The Food Web

In recent years, advances in soil ecology and microbiology have shown that most organisms living in the soil are integral to the survival and health of plants and that the key to preserving the fertility of soil is the maintenance of a diverse and healthy soil ecosystem, or food web. Conditions are good if your soil is moist, well aerated, and has a good supply of organic matter (bug food). You can also learn a lot about your soil just by digging around and seeing who's home.

Many soil organisms—such as bacteria and nematodes—can be seen only through the lens of a microscope, but a surprising number are visible to the naked eye. With the help of an identification guide, such as the wonderful *Life in the Soil*, by James Nardi, you can learn how to observe, trap, and identify the creatures in your soil—and understand the role each one plays in the food web.

Analyzing the Soil Food Web

For a more formal analysis of your soil food web, you can have your soil tested by a laboratory specializing in bioassays. These labs (see attra.ncat.org/attra-pub/soil-lab.html for a list) measure bacterial and fungal biomass and count organisms such as protozoa and nematodes—and they can tell you if any component of your food web is lacking. The tests are relatively expensive, costing upwards of $200 for a full soil food web analysis. Some of the methods prescribed for restoring specific parts of the food web to the soil—in particular, the use of aerated compost tea—are currently controversial because the preliminary research and data are inconclusive. In any case, you can look at it as an opportunity to field-test novel approaches in your own backyard.

WEEDS AS INDICATOR SPECIES?

Weeds growing in your garden may provide clues to conditions of your soil, such as fertility, pH, and texture. For instance, hawkweeds (*Hieracium* species) are known to prefer acidic soil. However, relying on weeds as the sole indicators of soil properties in your garden can be misleading, for a number of reasons.

Consistent populations of a single species (rather than a few individuals) need to be present for the clues to be meaningful. Moreover, most garden weeds can tolerate a wide range of soil conditions, so it may be difficult to draw any specific conclusions about your soil. Take dandelions, for instance: They are known to thrive in heavy clay soil, but they also like cultivated soils, as well as soils with low pH.

Many common weeds, such as dandelions, don't indicate any soil conditions in particular.

Conditioning Your Soil

Niall Dunne

Having investigated the texture, structure, and other physical conditions of your soil, what did you find out? Does it qualify as the textbook ideal—a rich, dark loam with a loose, granular structure? Is it crumbly, soft, and earthy smelling, friable but robust? Does it drain well yet retain sufficient moisture? If so, consider yourself in the minority. Most gardeners inherit soils that fall short of the golden mean—ones that are naturally somewhat clayey, sandy, thin, porous, or waterlogged or else have been disturbed, compacted, or depleted over time by human activities such as agriculture or construction.

At least two options are available to gardeners with not-so-delicious dirt. The simplest and most sustainable is to grow plants that will adapt to your soil's conditions. The second approach is to modify your soil to make the garden more hospitable to the plants you want to grow. There are several ways of doing this. The most expensive and energy intensive is to haul in truckloads of commercial topsoil (see "Shallow Soils," page 88). A less drastic option is to purchase a modest amount of topsoil, amend it with organic matter, and create islands of perfect planting medium in raised beds (see "Raised and Mounded Beds," page 98). Changing the soil you already have by mixing in conditioners is the most common approach.

Since ancient times, gardeners have used conditioners—also called amendments—to alter the physical properties of soil (in particular, its structure), with the aim of enhancing the soil's fitness for growing plants. When properly applied, conditioners help with aeration, permeability, and drainage. They improve the workability of heavy or compacted soils and increase the water-holding capacity of light, sandy soils—creating happier environments not only for plant roots but also for beneficial soil organisms. Conditioners can be divided into two broad categories: organic (derived from plant or animal residue) and mineral. In the sustainable garden—as in the gardens of old—organic conditioners produced with minimal energy from recycled or renewable local sources are the order of the day.

Improving Soil Quality

Organic soil conditioners are a gardener's best option for maintaining and improving soil quality. Along with enhancing soil structure, they act as slow-release fertilizers, providing a supplemental source of plant nutrients. And most of them can be sustainably produced. Organic conditioners have inherent physical qualities that immediately increase soil permeability and moisture retention. But they also provide a buffet dinner for soil organisms, which gradually improve soil structure and fertility

Organic soil conditioners like compost improve aeration, permeability, drainage, and workability of heavy or compacted soils and increase water-holding capacity of sandy soils.

Along with enhancing soil structure, organic conditioners such as the coir dust in this mounded bed act as slow-release fertilizers, providing a supplemental source of plant nutrients.

in myriad ways (see "Ecology of the Soil," page 14). The end product of organic matter decomposition—stable humus—is the key to the long-term health of your soil, providing good structure, aeration, moisture retention, and much more.

Gardeners are spoiled for choice when it comes to organics—most any plant residue can be used. Coarse, bulky composts and manures are ideal. You can also use high-carbon materials such as sawdust and shredded bark, but you should compost these prior to mixing them into the soil; otherwise, the soil microbes that digest them will temporarily draw down nitrogen levels in the soil, creating the potential for nutrient deficiencies in your plants. If you live in a dry or arid area with saline soil, avoid using manure or biosolids, which can have high salt content.

When preparing a new planting bed, the general rule is to work in about one inch of organic matter for every 4 to 6 inches of soil. (Don't overapply organic matter, as this can lead to nutrient loading of the soil and possible contamination of the environment, for example, through leaching of excess nutrients.) In general, if you intend to grow deep-rooted plants such as trees, shrubs, and grasses, you should amend your soil to a depth of about 12 to 18 inches. For herbaceous perennials and annuals, amending the soil to a depth of between 6 and 8 inches is usually sufficient.

The most sustainable way to mix in conditioners is by hand. This is best accomplished with a square-tined garden fork when the soil is moderately moist—digging in wet soil can cause compaction, and digging when the soil is too dry can break up its structure. Though more convenient—especially for preparing large planting beds—rotary tillers guzzle gas and cause much more damage to the hyphae of beneficial fungi than manual turning. If overused, tillers can also pulverize soil structure and create a layer of compaction below the rotating blades.

For established perennial beds and woody plants, digging in conditioners is not recommended—it can damage root systems and kill your plants. Instead, apply them to the soil surface as you would any organic mulch (see "The Magic of Mulch," page 68). This will gradually improve soil structure over time—earthworms and other soil creatures will incorporate the organic matter into the soil as it decomposes. Indeed, more and more gardeners these days are opting for a no-till approach to soil conditioning in all their planting beds—even ephemeral beds such as annual and vegetable gardens. This slower, more natural method of soil care favors beneficial soil organisms and also reduces the potential for soil erosion.

Organic Conditioners

Following is a selection of popular organic conditioners. Other good options include grass clippings, shredded leaves, and worm castings (from vermicomposting), which can all be produced at home. You can also investigate the local availability of mushroom compost, chopped straw, coffee grounds, and shredded buckwheat hulls.

Alfalfa Meal Ground alfalfa hay is a popular nitrogen fertilizer among organic growers and also makes a good conditioner, lightening clay soils and enhancing moisture retention in sandy soils. In addition, it stimulates microbial activity and contains the hormone triacontanol, which promotes plant growth.

Coir Dust Also called coco peat, coir dust is a by-product of the coir fiber industry, which processes coconut husks for their strong, decay-resistant tissues. Once it has been washed (to remove salt), the dust makes a highly effective soil conditioner and is marketed as an eco-friendly alternative to peat moss (see "For Peat's Sake," page 48). Coir dust improves soil aeration, water-holding capacity, and cation exchange capacity. It also contains root-stimulating hormones and a modest dose of nutrients (something lacking in peat). With a pH of 5.6 to 6.4, it is much less acidic than peat and compatible with a wider range of garden plants. Coir dust is usually sold in compressed blocks that need to be soaked in water before use.

Compost Without doubt the best and most sustainable conditioner of them all (you can make it in your own backyard!), compost rapidly improves soil tilth and nutrient availability. See "Compost: Homemade Humus for Healthy Soils," page 50.

Green Manure Grow your own organic matter by planting a cover crop in fall and working it into the soil in spring. Green manure is good for annual beds and vegetable gardens, as well as for preparing perennial beds. See "Green Manure," page 66.

Soil-conditioner samples from left to right: compost, coir dust, vermiculite, peat moss, perlite, and sand. Made from coconut-husk fibers, coir dust serves as an eco-friendly peat substitute.

Manure Most animal manures make good organic fertilizers and conditioners. It's cheaper and more sustainable to acquire manure from local farms and stables, but avoid material from sources that inject their animals with steroids or other medications or that spray larvicides to control flies. Before being used in the garden, manure should be composted thoroughly in a hot pile to reduce odor and kill off any bacterial pathogens, parasitic worms, or weed seeds that might be present.

Wastewater Sludge (Biosolids) A by-product of sewage treatment, wastewater sludge can be incorporated into garden soil as a source of organic matter and nutrients (in particular nitrogen, phosphorus, and a number of micronutrients). Using sludge—instead of landfilling it—closes a major loop in our enormous waste stream. The quality of biosolids has improved greatly during the last 30 years, and current biosolids do not present risk of harmful metal accumulation in the soil or uptake in the food chain. Biosolids do contain low levels of contaminants such as synthetic organics. Synthetic organics in biosolids have not been studied as thoroughly as metals, but current research suggests low risks of food-chain contamination by these compounds. The only biosolids permitted for use in gardens and landscapes are those that have been heat-treated or composted to meet Class A standards for pathogen reduction. Class A biosolids are suitable for all garden situations, but many people prefer to use them only on ornamental crops. (Certified organic growers are not permitted to use biosolids because of synthetic materials already present or added during wastewater treatment.)

Mineral Conditioners

Some naturally occurring inorganic substances are also used to condition soil. For instance, sand and perlite are added to clayey soil to physically modify its texture and improve drainage and airflow, and gypsum loosens up dense, high-sodium soils by chemically altering its structure. However, these conditioners are mined, nonrenewable resources, and their extraction is energy intensive and environmentally destructive. Sustainable gardeners should avoid or minimize their use of these products.

Gypsum Most often employed as a calcium and sulfur supplement, gypsum (calcium sulfate powder) is sometimes promoted as a conditioner for improving clayey soils. However, its effectiveness in these soils is debated. Gypsum is effective at aggregating high-sodium, or sodic, soils. These occur in small pockets in dry regions of the West and Midwest and have poor structure—the sodium ions react with clay particles, causing the soil aggregates to disperse, or come apart. Adding large amounts of gypsum (5 to 20 tons per acre) binds the soil into granular aggregates, improving aeration and drainage, and facilitates leaching of sodium from the soil using low-salt irrigation water (see "Saline Soils," page 90).

Lime Generally used as a calcium and magnesium supplement and to increase soil pH, ground limestone may also temporarily improve structure in clay soils by chemically transforming clay particles.

Sand Adding sand is an age-old panacea for improving drainage in tight, heavy soils. But to see lasting beneficial effects, you have to mix in roughly 50 percent of the stuff by volume into your soil. Also, the sand particles must be medium to coarse grained (0.25 to 1.0 millimeters in diameter); if they're any smaller, they'll clog up rather than enlarge pore spaces. Adding organic matter is a more effective and sensible way to loosen clayey soils.

Perlite and Vermiculite These minerals expand like popcorn when heated to form porous grains that can increase aeration and water retention in soils. Due to their cost, they're better suited for use in pots than in garden beds.

Usually applied in gardens to raise soil pH, lime may also help aggregate heavy clay soils.

FOR PEAT'S SAKE

SARAH REICHARD

Peat moss is partially decomposed organic matter extracted from sphagnum, hypnum, and reed-sedge bogs. The porous, spongy material has long been a preferred conditioner for increasing water-holding capacity, drainage, and humus levels in garden soils. And because of its low pH—ranging from 3.0 to 4.5 for sphagnum—peat is also used to increase soil acidity. However, peat's status as a renewable resource is hotly debated, and the material has generally fallen out of favor with conservation-minded gardeners.

Sphagnum peat moss is by far the most widely used of the various horticultural peats. It is made of any of a few hundred species in the genus *Sphagnum*, which grow primarily in temperate and cold-climate wetlands around the world. Most of the sphagnum peat moss used in North America comes from bogs in northern Canada. Sphagnum mosses are unusually resistant to decay. They also develop in low-oxygen and strongly acidic conditions, which further slow decomposition. As a result, deep layers of dead matter—up to several feet thick—accumulate underneath the living surface of sphagnum bogs.

Wetlands in general are very important for regulating surface-water flow and purity. Sphagnum bogs are important for additional reasons, including the fact that they are home to many rare plants and animals. Because the acidic and

To harvest peat, most of the water is drained from the bog, hampering regeneration.

Canadian sphagnum peat bogs, the source of most of the peat moss used in North America, are home to many rare animals and plants such as the purple pitcher plant.

low-oxygen conditions of sphagnum bogs slow decay, these wetlands are also important tools for studying the past. For example, bogs in northern Europe have preserved the bodies of people from thousands of years ago, giving us valuable information about how our ancestors lived. Pollen and seeds preserved at different depths in sphagnum bogs allow us to reconstruct the components and patterns of the vegetation over millennia. In addition, all peat wetlands have recently been recognized as important factors in the fight against global climate change—the amount of carbon stored in peat bogs at northern latitudes alone is only slightly less than that of all the living organisms on earth combined.

Harvesting peat involves draining a bog of about 95 percent of its water. This affects not only the area harvested but also reduces the water found in the surrounding bog. The growth rate of *Sphagnum* is very slow, and this in turn makes restoration of harvested sphagnum bogs extremely slow. What's more, preliminary studies suggest that regenerated wetlands tend to differ from original ones in their properties and composition—featuring, for example, many more trees and shrubs. Given all these caveats, sustainable gardeners should opt for more renewable conditioners when improving their soil. Good alternatives to peat include compost and horticultural-grade coir.

Compost: Homemade Humus for Healthy Soils

Grace Gershuny

Composting at home is a win-win endeavor. Not only do you create a wonderful source of organic matter for your soil, but you also close the recycling loop by diverting domestic waste from the landfill. According to the U.S. Environmental Protection Agency, a quarter of our solid-waste stream is made up of readily compostable yard trimmings and kitchen scraps. Municipal composting programs are starting up all over the country, and they are valuable enterprises worth supporting. But composting on-site saves transportation energy and overall is a much more satisfying experience.

Composting is the art and science of mixing various organic materials in a pile and controlling the conditions so that soil organisms break down the raw organic matter into humus. It mimics the natural humus-formation processes that take place whenever leaves fall or plants die. High-quality humus—the dark, fragrant, spongy material often referred to as black gold or gardener's gold—is the cornerstone of soil health, providing good structure to the soil, food and living quarters for soil critters, and a modest source of slow-release nutrients to plants. In addition to humus, well-made compost is also laden with beneficial microbes that have been shown to protect plants from soil-borne pathogens and produce growth-stimulating compounds.

Complex chemical and biological processes are involved in transforming raw organic material into finished compost. Compost ecosystems consist of vast numbers and types of organisms, whose interactions are still only slightly known. Macrofauna—creatures such as mites, millipedes, springtails, beetles, ants, flies, nematodes, and most importantly, earthworms—set the stage by physically breaking down the raw materials through biting, chewing, sucking, and grinding them and excreting what is left after passage through their digestive tracts. Microfauna—in particular bacteria and fungi—then take over to complete the process of decomposition. The end product (humus) is a blend of complex organic compounds of plant, animal, and microbial origin that are relatively resistant to further decay.

The principal task of the gardener who wants to compost at home is to provide the best possible conditions for the microherd to flourish and reproduce. These conditions include a balanced supply of moisture and air and the right proportions of different types of organic matter.

Composting is an easy way to dispose of plant-based kitchen scraps and yard waste locally and generate a top-notch soil conditioner right in your backyard or community garden.

Moisture and Air

The organisms in your compost pile need water in order to digest their food. Ideal water content is somewhere between 50 and 70 percent. When you squeeze the compost in your hand, it should feel damp but not dripping wet—like a wrung-out sponge. If there's too much moisture, air won't be able to circulate properly through the pile, and anaerobic bacteria will start to dominate the microherd and produce putrid odors. Adding bulky materials and routinely, or at least occasionally, turning the pile will guarantee a good supply of oxygen for the aerobic microbes you want working on your compost.

Organic Ingredients and Nutrient Balances

The fungi and bacteria in your pile need a balanced diet. It should contain a carbon-to-nitrogen ratio (C:N) of around 30:1 by weight. You don't need to worry too much about the math, just as long as you include a mix of high-carbon materials ("brown" or dry stuff, such as straw, fall leaves, newspaper, and sawdust) and high-nitrogen materials ("green" or wet stuff, such as grass clippings, kitchen scraps, and fresh cuttings from the garden). Two common items found in most compost piles are tree leaves and grass clippings. Tree leaves have a C:N ratio between 40:1 and 80:1, while grass clippings have a ratio of 20:1; so an equal combination of the two should give you the right proportions. However, try to vary your pile's ingredients as much as possible, as this diversifies the microhabitats for the decomposers in the pile and helps create more nutrient-rich compost.

Cold composting requires little in the way of equipment or maintenance: Pile a mixture of ingredients together as they become available, and then leave the heap alone.

Though everything eventually will decompose, the brown items generally provide your pile with bulk and aeration, while the green ones provide the microorganisms with an easily digestible source of energy. An even mix of browns and greens also encourages a healthy balance of fungi (which are better at digesting cellulose and lignin) and bacteria (which break down substrates such as starches and proteins). Some composting books recommend alternating thick layers of brown materials with thin layers of green materials in your pile. However, this layering practice is unnecessary and may create zones of anaerobic activity in the green layers and inactivity in the brown.

If you've had your soil analyzed and know that it's lacking in some nutrients, you can also sprinkle in some rock minerals whenever you add fresh organic matter. This technique incorporates the slow-release nutrients in the rock powders into the humus and makes them more readily available to plants. Common supplements for the compost pile include greensand or granite dust (for potassium, calcium, and magnesium) and bonemeal or rock phosphate (for phosphorus and calcium). For supplementing micronutrients, rich sources include seaweed or kelp meal. You can also purchase a batch of aged manure to supplement nutrients in your garden rather than experiment with various bags of mined rock powders.

What Not to Add to the Compost Pile

Materials that are not of plant or animal origin, with the exception of small amounts of mined minerals, should not be used in compost. Avoid meat scraps, bones, grease, or whole eggs, which can cause unpleasant odors and attract rodents. Don't add any feces from pets—they can harbor pathogens harmful to infants and pregnant women. And steer clear of sawdust from pressure-treated lumber and plywood, which can contain harmful levels of arsenic. Don't use grass clippings or yard waste that may have been treated with herbicides, as some are known to suppress compost organisms and can even damage garden plants because they don't break down during composting.

Siting and Protecting the Pile

Locate your pile away from wooden walls or fences, which may come under attack from compost fungi. Choose a well-drained location, where your pile won't be subject to standing water. A base of wood chips or coarse residues such as brush or cornstalks will allow water to drain through easily and increase aeration. Too much water passing through the pile will leach away soluble nutrients; in humid climates, protect the pile from excess moisture, either by placing the pile under a shelter or by covering it. A plastic or canvas tarpaulin should only be used once compost is finished, but a cover layer of hay or straw will shed water without stopping air penetration. If you're not enclosing your pile in a compost bin, it's a good idea to screen or fence it off to protect it from foraging by wildlife or neighboring pets.

How to Compost

There are two basic ways to make compost: the slow way (also called cold, passive, or lazy composting) and the fast way (also called hot composting). It's up to you to decide which method suits your needs, schedule, or budget. Each has its pros and cons (see the box at the bottom of this page). For instance, cold composting results in higher nitrogen content than hot, while hot composting kills weed seeds and disease organisms that may persist after the cold process.

Cold Composting This is simple, requiring little in the way of equipment or maintenance. In short: Just pile all your ingredients together as they become available until you've got a good-size heap (four to five feet in diameter and about three feet high), and then leave the heap alone. In a year or two, you'll have finished compost, at least at the bottom of the pile.

The maximum temperature that cold compost reaches is about 120°F, which is not hot enough to kill weed seeds or plant pathogens. However, there is evidence that cold compost contains more beneficial fungi, which tend to proliferate at cooler temperatures and are slower growing and less tolerant of disturbance.

Some Like It Hot Hot composting is a more involved process, demanding much greater attention to balancing your raw materials and regulating aeration and moisture. Get everything right, and the microorganism populations in your pile will go into a feeding and growth frenzy, accelerating the decomposition process to such an extent that finished compost can be produced within four to eight weeks. As the microbes consume the organic matter, they release heat. Temperatures rise quickly, and a succession of mesophilic (moderate-heat-loving) and thermophilic (high-heat-

HOT COMPOSTING		COLD COMPOSTING	
PROS	CONS	PROS	CONS
Kills pathogens, fly larvae, and weed seeds	Labor intensive	Low maintenance	Nutrients can be lost through prolonged exposure to elements
Produces finished compost relatively quickly	Releases more nitrogen through volatilization	Conserves nitrogen	Takes more time before usable
Product is well decomposed and uniform	Not as effective at suppressing plant pathogens	More hospitable for plant-pathogen-suppressing organisms (fungi and nematodes)	Doesn't kill pathogens or weed seeds
			Finished product may be inconsistent, with undecomposed high-carbon materials that require screening

Hot composting requires at least a cubic yard of brown and green ingredients in just the right proportions to start. The pile has to be monitored closely and turned and watered as needed.

loving) microbes thrive in the pile. Peak temperature can reach between 130°F and 150°F (or higher in very large piles) within a couple of days. Now that's pretty hot!

For hot compost, you need to assemble at least a cubic yard of organic matter to start your pile. If the pile is any smaller than that, it may not be able to trap enough heat. Air and water control are two sides of the same coin: Too much moisture reduces aeration, while too much air dries out the pile too quickly.

The best way to control moisture is to start with a good balance of wet (green) and dry (brown) ingredients and mix them well. Adding water as you build or turn the pile is also helpful. Use the squeeze test to determine moisture content. If it's too low, add more water; if it's too high, aerate, or if necessary, add more dry material.

You can supply good airflow by turning the pile (moving the inner material to the outside and vice versa) or mixing it about once a week. It's easier to do this if you own a compost tumbler or a bin with multiple chambers. Shredding the raw materials before you add them to the pile increases aeration and provides more surface area for microbes to munch on. You can also enhance aeration by building your pile on a foundation of coarse organic materials such as brush.

Too much air can sometimes be a problem, drying the pile to the point where microbial activity slows down. The simplest solution to excess aeration, as you may have guessed already, is to add water, either by hosing down the pile or by turning the pile and periodically wetting it as you rebuild it.

A good-size, well-maintained hot compost pile will take about three to five days to reach the optimal temperature range, between 130°F and 150°F. If this temperature is maintained for three or more days, pathogens, fly larvae, and weed seeds will be destroyed. Macrofauna such as worms survive this thermophilic phase by moving to the cooler edges of the pile and going dormant. Once the compost begins to cool, it can be turned, and this will cause the temperature to rise again due to increased oxygen and exposure of previously buried materials. Eventually, turning generates no further heat, and you can allow the compost to sit for several weeks to mature, or cure, by the action of numerous beneficial mesophilic microorganisms that recolonize the pile.

Using Finished Compost

When your compost is finished, the total mass of the pile will be reduced by about half. The original materials will be indistinguishable, and the compost will have a relatively uniform color and texture along with a pleasant, earthy smell. Bits of coarse carbonaceous materials like wood chips or corncobs may still remain, and these can either be screened out or left in the mix to add undigested organic matter to the soil. Coarse compost is fine for working into the soil before transplanting vegetables or flowers or for top-dressing perennial beds, trees, and shrubs. Potting mixes and seedbeds for crops like carrots require screened compost.

Good-quality finished compost is highly versatile. It can be applied to any crop or ornamental plant, at any time. Digging in or top-dressing with an inch or two of compost per year is the general recommendation. Though mature compost is an incomparable soil conditioner and a valuable source of nutrients (with an average nitrogen, phosphorus, and potassium equivalent of 1-1-1), perhaps its primary value is as a soil inoculant, stimulating greater biological activity and release of nutrients for plants. Accordingly, the best results come from spreading the available compost thinly over a large area rather than concentrating it in a smaller area.

During composting, the total mass of your ingredients reduces by about half. Depending on method and management, the hot process may take 8 to 12 weeks and the cold a year or more.

COMPOST TEA

Not too long ago, gardeners discovered the benefits of compost tea. All you had to do to make it was put some compost in a burlap sack and steep it in water for a while. The end product was a rich liquid infusion that could be used as a foliar spray or root drench to give your plants a healthful—though very modest—dose of mineral nutrients and other beneficial compounds.

In recent years, compost tea has become much more high tech—and big business. Commercial enterprises selling both compost tea and equipment for brewing compost tea have proliferated like flies on a manure pile. The focus has shifted away from creating liquid fertilizer to breeding various microbial cultures and using them to enhance the ecological health of garden soils.

Today's probiotic tea makers start off with a liquid extract similar to the compost teas of old, but they use machines to pump in lots of air, to stimulate growth of resident aerobic bacteria and fungi and to separate the microbes out from the compost matter. They also add microbial food sources to the brew, further increasing the size of the microherd. The finished product—actively aerated compost tea (AACT)—is used as a foliar spray or soil drench not only to provide soluble nutrients but also to establish diverse microbial populations, thereby boosting soil-nutrient cycling, suppressing plant pathogens, and improving soil structure.

Or at least that's what AACT advocates claim it can do. However, the evidence so far is mostly anecdotal. Research on the supposed benefits of AACT is still in the preliminary stages, and the results of trials investigating AACT's disease-suppressing abilities have been mixed at best. Ongoing studies at Penn State and other universities have shown AACT to be somewhat effective at battling the soil-borne pathogen gray mold, but—so far—it appears ineffective against a host of other diseases. (It's also been shown to be somewhat effective against powdery mildew, but this is no breakthrough; nonaerated compost tea used as a foliar spray is already known to reduce the incidence of plant foliar diseases.)

Critics also argue that unless your soil is already hospitable to soil microorganisms, inoculation with microbial teas is a waste of time, because the microbes probably won't survive. They add that you're much better off just applying good compost, which not only inoculates the soil with beneficial organisms but also improves the physical environment in which they live and gives them a rich supply of carbon on which to feed.

But it's early days yet for this new technology. If you have the inclination, why not conduct your own research on AACT? Detailed instructions for making and customizing AACT for your plants are available at soilfoodweb.com, the website of Dr. Elaine Ingham, the guru of probiotic compost tea.

Fertilizing Your Garden

Craig Cogger

Improving the physical, chemical, and biological properties of your soil using organic conditioners and mulches is the most effective and sustainable way to build up its long-term natural fertility. However, if your plants start to show signs of nutrient deficiency (see "The Essential Minerals," page 30), and a soil test confirms it, you will need—at least in the short term—to supplement your soil's native nutrient supply with fertilizer.

Many fertilizers are available on the market. Any one of them should be used cautiously and sparingly. Overuse or misapplication of fertilizer can injure plants and soil organisms, create nutrient imbalances in the soil, and lead to pollution of waterways. The goal of sustainable nutrient management is to meet the nutrient needs of your plants while conserving resources, improving soil health, and protecting water quality. There are a number of things you can do to achieve this goal in the garden, such as choosing fertilizers made from recycled natural materials over synthetic products whenever possible.

Natural and Synthetic Fertilizers

Fertilizers fall into two general groups: natural and synthetic. Natural fertilizers are those that have undergone little or no processing. They include both biological (plant and animal) and mineral materials. Although they are often referred to as organic because they are generally certified for use in organic farming, in this book we use the term "natural" because "organic" (which in scientific parlance means simply "containing carbon") is used to denote "derived from plants or animals" only.

Once in the soil, natural fertilizers release nutrients in soluble ionic form through biological decomposition and mineral weathering. Compared with synthetic fertilizers, they usually have a lower concentration of the primary nutrients nitrogen (N), phosphorus (P), and potassium (K). Thus, larger amounts of natural fertilizers may be needed to supply the "big three." However, since natural fertilizers release their nutrients more slowly, the effects last longer, and there is less risk of nutrient leaching. In addition, natural fertilizers often contain supplies of secondary nutrients and micronutrients generally not found in synthetics.

Natural fertilizers include materials with a wide range of nutrient contents, nutrient availability, and handling characteristics. Examples include animal manures; animal by-products such as fish, feather, and bone meals; seed meals; and minerals such as rock phosphate. Many natural fertilizers are recycled from materials that

Fertilizers come in many guises: Frost-tender buckwheat can be planted in spring or summer to serve as a warm-season cover crop that enriches the soil and suppresses weeds.

Liquid fertilizers such as seaweed emulsion or compost tea can be used in foliar sprays and drenches. Dilute the emulsion in water and apply it early in the morning or on a cloudy day.

would otherwise be discarded as wastes. The production of synthetic fertilizers, on the other hand, usually results in the creation of wastes.

Choosing among natural fertilizers involves trade-offs in cost and convenience. For instance, farmyard manure usually is inexpensive or free but can be inconvenient to obtain, cure, and apply; packaged natural blends are convenient but often expensive. The choice also involves issues of sustainability—in particular when it comes to deciding between nonrenewable mined substances (whose extraction is energy intensive and environmentally destructive) and recycled plant or animal material.

Synthetic fertilizers are manufactured or are refined from natural ingredients to make them more concentrated and more available to plants. Typically, they are processed into soluble ionic forms (such as salts) that are immediately available to plants. Some synthetic fertilizers are further processed to slow the rate of nutrient release, mimicking organic fertilizers. These include coated, slow-release pellets used for potted or container plants and "synthetic organic" fertilizers, such as methylene urea polymers used for lawns.

The source of nitrogen in synthetic fertilizers is nitrogen gas from the atmosphere. The manufacturing process is the chemical equivalent of biological nitrogen fixation but requires enormous amounts of fossil fuel energy. Synthetic phosphorus fertilizers come from phosphate rock. The rock is treated with acid to release phosphorus into plant-available forms. The most common raw material for potassium fertilizers is sylvinite, an ore containing potassium chloride salts mined from beds deep within the earth.

Nutrient Availability

Because most synthetic fertilizers supply immediately available nutrients, they can be effective in early spring, before the soil is warm. However, nitrogen in these fertilizers is vulnerable to leaching loss from heavy rainfall or irrigation. Once nitrogen moves below the root zone, plants can no longer use it, and it may leach into groundwater and harm water quality. If applying synthetic, soluble sources of nitrogen to plants with a large nitrogen demand and long season of uptake (such as turfgrass), it is best to split fertilizing into multiple applications to reduce the potential for leaching. Phosphorus and potassium do not leach as readily as nitrogen because they are more quickly bound up in the soil.

Nutrients in most natural fertilizers become available to plants during the course of the growing season. The rate of release of available nitrogen depends on both the type of material and the environment. Nitrogen-rich materials such as fish fertilizer, broiler litter (poultry bedding and manure), feather meal, and seed meals decompose relatively quickly under warm, moist conditions, releasing substantial amounts of nitrogen and other nutrients within a few weeks of application, followed by slower release thereafter. Most composted organic materials (made from yard debris, cattle manure, etc.) decompose much more slowly, releasing only about 5 percent of their total nitrogen during the growing season. Repeated application builds up a pool of slow-release nutrients that, in the long run, decreases the need for supplemental fertilizer. Note that natural fertilizers will continue to release nutrients in warm weather whether or not plants are present. Vegetable gardeners who harvest plants early in the season should grow a cover crop on any bare soil to prevent leaching. See also "Green Manure," page 66, and "Vegetables," page 110.

Fertilizer Labels

The labels on processed fertilizer packages tell you the amount of each of the three primary nutrients in the fertilizer, expressed as a percentage of total fertilizer weight. Nitrogen (N) is always listed first, phosphorus (P) second, and potassium (K) third. Thus, a bag of fertilizer labeled 5-10-10 contains 5 percent nitrogen, 10 percent phosphorus (expressed as units of phosphorus pentoxide, P_2O_5), and 10 percent potassium (expressed as units of potash, K_2O). This information is called a fertilizer analysis. The analysis for synthetic fertilizers guarantees the amount of available nutrients in the fertilizer. The analysis for natural fertilizers represents the total amount of nutrients rather than immediately available nutrients.

Micronutrients

Micronutrient deficiencies are much less common than macronutrient deficiencies. They are most often related to high alkalinity (see "Understanding Soil pH," page 28) but can also occur in coarse, sandy soils that are low in organic matter. Do not routinely add micronutrient supplements to garden or landscape soils! If you suspect micronutrient problems, have your soil tested and make pH adjustments or micronutrient additions accordingly. Renewable, organic sources of micronutrients include kelp meal and alfalfa meal.

Applying Fertilizers

The goal of applying fertilizer (whether the source is natural or synthetic) is to supply enough nutrients to meet plant needs without accumulating excess nutrients in the soil that could leach into groundwater or run off into surface water. Soil testing (see "Getting to Know Your Soil," page 34) is the best way to estimate fertilizer needs based on the specific conditions in your yard and garden. Soil-testing labs also provide tips, techniques, and timing for recommended fertilizer applications.

Calculating Synthetic Fertilizer Amounts

Fertilizer recommendations are usually given in pounds of nutrient (such as the three primaries, expressed collectively as NPK) per unit area (typically 100 or 1,000 square feet for gardens). You will need to convert the pounds of nutrient to pounds of fertilizer. For example, say your soil test results indicate that you should add two pounds of N per 1,000 square feet of garden using a fertilizer with a 1:1:1 ratio of NPK. The first step is to choose a fertilizer with the correct proportions, such as 8-8-8 (rather than a 21-4-4). Then calculate how much 8-8-8 is needed for 1,000 square feet by dividing the amount of N recommended (two pounds) by the fraction of N in the fertilizer (8 percent or 0.08):

$$2 \text{ lb.} \div 0.08 = 25 \text{ lb. per 1,000 square feet}$$

Then simply calculate the area of your garden (in square feet) and the amount of fertilizer needed for it.

Calculating Natural Fertilizer Amounts

Determining how much natural fertilizer to use often involves an extra step, because you must estimate the availability of the nutrients (particularly nitrogen). Research done in the Pacific Northwest showed a relationship between the nitrogen concentration and rate of nitrogen release for uncomposted natural fertilizers such as fresh manures and packaged seed and animal by-product meals. (See page 65 for profiles and nutrient contents of some common natural fertilizers.) Natural fertilizers with large proportions of nitrogen (greater than 6 percent), such as blood meal and cottonseed meal, release roughly three-quarters of their nitrogen over the growing season and may be substituted for synthetic fertilizers almost on a one-to-one basis. Natural fertilizers with 3 to 5 percent nitrogen (such as fish emulsion) release roughly half of their nitrogen during the season—so you need to double up on them to get the same amount of nitrogen you would get from a synthetic product in a single growing season. In climates that are hotter than the Northwest, where these figures were derived, the rate of nutrient release from natural fertilizers will be faster.

Fortunately, more and more soil labs are providing natural fertilizer calculations, and most packaged and processed natural fertilizers feature helpful guidelines for rate application. Unpackaged materials can contain a considerable amount of moisture that further dilutes the nutrients. Typical application rates for chicken manure (including moisture) are in the range of 3 to 5 gallons per 100 square feet of garden, while one for rabbit-manure fertilizer ranges from 20 to 40 gallons per 100 square feet. After application, observe your plants carefully. Lush growth and delayed flowering and fruiting are signs of high amounts of available nitrogen and may indicate overfertilization.

When to Fertilize

In general, add fertilizer based on the performance of your plants. If they display a lack of vigor, retarded growth, sparse foliage, discoloration of leaves, and twig dieback, have your soil tested. It's more likely than not that your plants' problems are related to drainage and aeration, but a soil test will provide certainty. If your soil is lacking nutrients, in most cases, the best time to apply fertilizer is close to the time when plants need the nutrients the most. This reduces the potential for nutrient loss and environmental contamination.

Timing of application is more important when using synthetics. Nutrient release from natural fertilizer is generally in sync with plant demands, because microbial activity necessary for its release more or less matches plant activity during the season.

Plants need the largest amount of nutrients when they are growing most rapidly, generally in spring. But get to know your plants, because growth cycles can vary widely. For instance, cool-season grasses benefit from a fertilizer application in early fall, when their roots reactivate after a relatively stressful period in summer.

Many natural fertilizers such as Zoo Doo are recycled from materials that might otherwise be discarded as waste.

Plants need a lot of nutrients shortly after seeding or transplanting. For example, young plants establishing their root systems generally have higher phosphorus needs than mature plants. Because climate and growing season vary across North America, the best timing for fertilizer applications also varies. Refer to local sources such as Cooperative Extension publications to learn more (see bbg.org/soils for more information).

Fertilizer Tips for "Greener" Gardens

- Have your soil tested to determine if you need to add supplemental nutrients; choose renewable organic fertilizers (preferably ones produced locally) over synthetic or mined products whenever possible.

- Use single-nutrient fertilizers instead of complete fertilizers (ones that contain NPK) whenever appropriate. For instance, if your soil test says you have high levels of P and K but low N, use nitrogen-fixing legumes or a single-element fertilizer like fish emulsion or blood meal.

- Apply the recommended amount of fertilizer at the time of year the plant is most likely to use it. Contact your county Cooperative Extension agent for specific advice.

- Use slow-release fertilizers, or split applications of fast-release materials, to reduce the potential for nitrogen loss.

- Sweep stray fertilizer particles from the pavement into the garden.

- Create unfertilized buffer zones next to streams or drainage ways to reduce the risk of contaminating runoff.

- Plant winter cover crops in vegetable and annual beds or when preparing perennial beds. See "Green Manure," on page 66.

- Compost your yard trimmings and kitchen waste and apply it to your soil to increase organic matter and thus improve structure, soil nutrient supply, and water-holding capacity.

Composting puts kitchen scraps and yard waste to good use, returning nutrients to the soil in a slow-release form.

Natural Fertilizers

Following is a selection of common natural fertilizers. They are certified for use in organic gardening, but not all of them qualify as sustainable. The production of mined fertilizers such as rock phosphate, for instance, is energy intensive and environmentally destructive, and it involves the depletion of a nonrenewable resource. Fertilizers that are recycled by-products of industry—such as blood meal and fish emulsion—are more sustainable. However, they can only be truly sustainable if the farms and fisheries they're derived from are managed carefully, humanely, and ecologically. When it comes to choosing a fertilizer for your garden, look for local, renewable organic products that have been sustainably produced or harvested.

Alfalfa Pellets Manufactured primarily for feed, as a fertilizer alfalfa pellets offer nitrogen and potassium, trace minerals, and the growth-stimulating hormone triacontanol. Typical NPK: 2-0.5-2

Blood Meal Made from dried slaughterhouse waste, blood meal is very high in nitrogen (and can burn plants if overapplied). Typical NPK: 12-1-1

Bonemeal A slaughterhouse by-product very high in phosphorus and calcium, bonemeal gradually raises pH, so it's best used in acidic soils. Typical NPK: 1-12-0

Broiler Litter A by-product of the poultry industry made up of poultry manure along with organic bedding material (wood shavings, straw, and dry matter), feathers, and spilled feed, broiler litter is relatively bulky, so try to source locally. Typical NPK: 4-4-5

Cottonseed Meal A by-product of cotton mills, it is high in nitrogen and tends to decrease soil pH. It may contain residual pesticides. Typical NPK: 6-2-1

Fish Emulsion Created from the fluid remains of commercial fish production, fish emulsion is rich in nitrogen and micronutrients. Typical NPK: 3-1-1

Fish Meal Fish parts or rejected whole fish are ground and dried to make a fertilizer that is high in nitrogen and tends to increase soil pH. Typical NPK: 5-3-3

Kelp Meal This extract of seaweed is valued for its micronutrients and growth hormones; it contains modest amounts of nitrogen and potassium. Typical NPK: 1-0.1-2

Greensand A sandstone-based fertilizer mined from marine deposits in the coastal Northeast, it adds potassium and many trace minerals to soil. Typical NPK: 0-0-3

Rock phosphate Derived from prehistoric marine deposits quarried in Florida, Idaho, and elsewhere, rock phosphate is high in phosphate and calcium. It raises pH and is best used in acidic soils. Typical NPK: 0-25-0

GREEN MANURE

Cover crops, grown to protect bare soil from raindrop impact and erosion, capture nutrients leaching through the root zone, compete with weeds, and add organic matter to the soil after they are incorporated, are often referred to as green manure. Legumes grown for this purpose also provide fixed nitrogen for the following year's plants. Green manure crops are typically grains or grasses such as rye, oats, or annual ryegrass; legumes such as clovers, vetches, cowpeas, or fava beans; or a mixture of both. Refer to Cooperative Extension publications or other reliable local sources for the best cover crop varieties and preferred planting dates for your area. Avoid plants that are listed as invasive in your region.

Most gardeners plant green manure crops in the fall to provide winter cover for vegetable and annual beds and fresh organic matter in the spring. The key to having good winter cover is to plant early—usually in September in northern climates. Later plantings result in much less winter cover but will still produce substantial biomass in the spring.

Growing cereal or grass crops together with legumes provides multiple benefits to your garden. A robust green manure with legumes can supply half or more of the nitrogen needed for the following crop. Inoculating the legume seed with commercially available *Rhizobia*—the bacteria responsible for nitrogen fixation in legumes (see "The Nitrogen Cycle," page 33)—may increase nitrogen availability.

The biomass of the cover crops increases in the spring up to the point of flowering. After flowering, the green manure declines in quality. For best results, incorporate the cover crops in the spring before flowering, and wait two to three weeks to allow initial decomposition before planting. Some gardeners mow their cover crops and use them as mulch, transplanting directly into the mulch residue. This method reduces the biomass contribution of the cover crop, but it also reduces soil disturbance and weeds.

TIPS FOR PLANTING AND TURNING UNDER

- To get them off to a good start, plant winter-hardy crops at least four weeks before the expected date for the first hard frost in your area.

- Plant crops with large seeds like peas in shallow closely spaced furrows. Broadcast crops with small seeds like rye on top of the soil and cover them lightly by raking.

- If the weather is dry, water your cover crop to keep the soil slightly moist.

- In spring turn the crop under three weeks before you want to plant to give the organic matter time to start breaking down.

Gardeners most often plant cover crops in beds where vegetables or annuals were cultivated during the growing season. Cover crops protect the bare soil from the impact of rain and erosion and replenish soil nutrients.

The Magic of Mulch

Janet Marinelli

When it comes to mulching, like almost everything else I do in my garden, I try to think like a forest. Forests are the most biologically productive and diverse terrestrial habitats, so I figure they're good role models. Prairies and other plant communities generate layers of organic litter, but forests, especially deciduous forests, are nature's ultimate mulching machines.

Each autumn, deciduous trees relinquish summer's trappings in a rain of blazing foliage. Leaves contain a good deal of the forest's biomass, and also many of the nutrients essential for growth that tree roots pluck from the soil. As the fallen leaves slowly decay, their nutrients are released by bacteria, fungi, and other microorganisms, and they are transformed into food for the plant community. They also provide food and habitat for larger soil organisms, such as earthworms, which are eaten in turn by birds and other small animals. The blanket of organic matter insulates the soil, protecting the plants from extremes of temperature. It prevents soil from eroding away with storm water or wind and conserves precious soil moisture that otherwise would evaporate readily into the atmosphere.

Mulching can have all these advantages in the garden—and more. However, not all mulches are equally beneficial, and some can have environmental effects that are downright destructive. For example, recent reports have documented how the growing demand by gardeners for cypress mulch has led to increased logging in endangered cypress swamps that provide critical flood control, particularly in Louisiana and Florida. Fortunately, many environment-friendly mulches are available, and the "greenest" and most inexpensive mulch often can be found right in your own backyard.

Garden Benefits

Mulch's ability to conserve water in the garden has long been recognized—no small matter when you consider that 30 percent of municipal water in the eastern U.S. goes to irrigate gardens (in the West this figure is 60 percent). A blanket of mulch keeps the soil around your plants' roots from frying in summer, and in winter it helps prevent the soil from alternately freezing and thawing, which leads to soil heaving and root damage. By cushioning the impact of pounding rainfall, mulch also hampers soil compaction. Rain runs right off the surface of rock-hard ground, but loose soil allows water to penetrate and plant roots to breathe. Over time, organic mulches, those made of plant material, decompose and add organic matter to your soil, improving even more its ability to retain water and sustain the soil fauna that convert them into nutrients.

Mulch conserves water, moderates soil temperatures, and cushions the impact of rainfall. Used as a living mulch, clover captures nitrogen and makes it available to the corn when it needs it.

Stone mulches are great for rock gardens and are an attractive and regionally appropriate choice for gardens in dry climates, where organic mulches may constitute a fire hazard.

Mulch not only creates conditions in which plants are less stressed and more vigorous, and therefore less vulnerable to pests and diseases, but also eliminates the need for hours of backbreaking work. It suppresses weeds. And since it keeps the soil loose, there's no need for repeated cultivation with hoe or scuffle.

What to Look For

The best mulches are both light and open enough to permit water and air to penetrate to the soil and substantial enough to inhibit the growth of weeds. Mulches are either inorganic or organic.

Inorganic Mulches Inorganic mulches, including crushed stone, gravel, plastics, and recycled rubber chips, are not made of plant material, but they can still play an important part in the garden. Stone and gravel mulches are great for rock gardens, driveways, and pathways. They can also be a more appropriate choice for gardens in dry or arid regions, where organic mulches may constitute a fire hazard or be difficult to produce locally in large quantities. Black plastic mulch can be useful in the vegetable garden, in particular for warming up soils in springtime. Rubber mulch recycled from car tires may not be appropriate for landscaping due to high levels of metal and organic contaminants.

Organic Mulches In most climates and situations, organic mulches are preferable to inorganic ones for planting beds because they eventually break down and enrich the soil. A mind-boggling array of bagged organic mulches is available. But you can save yourself some serious money, and also make your garden function more eco-logically, by mulching fallen leaves from your own property. In the typical home garden, leaves and lawn clippings are bagged up and shipped off to the local landfill, accounting for more than 13 percent by weight of all municipal solid waste generated in the U.S.—an astonishing 32 million tons a year—according to a 2005 study by the Environmental Protection Agency. To compensate for these lost nutrients, gardeners buy fertilizers synthesized using fossil fuels that date back to before the days of the dinosaurs. By contrast, forests are "closed-loop" natural systems. Leaves fall to the ground, decompose, and become plant food.

If you have some large trees on your property, you can use the fallen leaves, nature's favorite mulching material, in your landscape. Whole leaves tend to mat together and block the movement of water into the soil, so before applying them to your planting beds, shred them with an electric leaf shredder, or simply pass over them with your lawn mower (you'll save yourself the trouble of raking if you attach the grass catcher first). Pine needles from any pine trees on your property are another great source of mulch.

If you need more mulch than you can produce from your garden, check with local arborists to see if they can supply you with free wood chips recycled from their daily prunings. When purchasing commercial mulch, avoid products made from species of conservation concern, such as cypress. To be sure you're buying a mulch that is a recycled by-product of timber operations and not made from whole

trees felled solely for the manufacture of mulch, look for products expressly labeled "bark mulch," not just wood or hardwood mulch. Bark mulches must contain at least 85 percent bark.

Be aware, too, that hardwood mulch can contain recycled construction and demolition debris treated with chromated copper arsenate (CCA), which means it is contaminated with arsenic, a human carcinogen. CCA is no longer utilized to treat most residential wood products, but was used for decades in the manufacture of pressure-treated wood to resist rot. To make sure you are not purchasing hardwood mulch contaminated with arsenic, look for

Lightweight and pliable, straw works well around plants with delicate stems.

products certified by the Mulch & Soil Council, a trade group. Certified mulch is tested chemically to ensure that it contains no CCA-treated wood. Among the other advantages of buying certified mulch is that you can be sure that the product label accurately represents what's in the bag—that, for example, a bag labeled bark mulch is indeed bark.

Some research has shown that high-carbon mulches such as bark or wood chips can temporarily draw down nitrogen levels in the soil as they decompose, "robbing" it from your plants. However, I have used bark mulches on my woody plants and herbaceous perennials for years and have never observed any adverse effects. If you are concerned about woody mulches causing nitrogen deficiencies in your plants, top-dress your soil with a thin layer of compost or aged manure before applying them.

A variety of organic by-products available locally also make excellent mulches—and recycle material that might otherwise be disposed of as waste. Midwestern gardeners have long reaped the benefits of mulch made from the ground-up corncobs so readily available in the region. Pecan shells and cottonseed and peanut hulls in the South, cranberry vines from Cape Cod and Wisconsin bogs, and spent hops from local breweries nationwide are among the many good candidates for mulching. So is a thin layer of coffee grounds from your own coffee machine or the neighborhood café.

Look also for mulches made from invasive trees in your area—for example, melaleuca mulch, which is now commercially available in Florida. First brought to the state from Australia about a hundred years ago, melaleuca (*Melaleuca quinquenervia*) proceeded to colonize an estimated 20 percent of all natural lands south of Lake Okeechobee,

Nature makes the most of mulch: As fallen leaves decay on the forest floor, their nutrients are released by bacteria, fungi, and other microorganisms and become available to plants.

choking out native species. Mulches from eradication efforts have the biggest environmental benefits of all: They not only have the horticultural advantages of other organic materials but also encourage the removal and recycling of invasive trees that are destroying native habitats. Just be sure they've been hot composted before bagging in order to kill any stray seeds. See page 74 for more ideas.

How to Lay It On

As a rule of thumb, most mulches should be about three inches deep for best results, although this varies to some extent, depending on the type of mulch. The finer the material, the thinner the layer should be; a mulch of coffee grounds, for example, should be no more than an inch thick.

How *not* to lay it on: Piling up mulch against tree trunks promotes decay and provides cover for bark-nibbling rodents.

Optimum mulch depth also depends on the type of soil it's intended for. Sandy soil, which loses moisture rapidly, benefits from a thicker mulch than clay soil, which tends to retain water. To avoid diseases, animal predation, and other problems, never pile mulch "volcano style" against tree trunks or plant stems; instead, pull it back an inch or two. Before applying mulch, remove any existing weeds, then water well.

Timing is everything. To be most effective, spread mulch around heat-loving vegetables like peppers and tomatoes after the soil has warmed—in mid- or late spring in most areas. Cabbages, greens, and other cool-weather crops can be mulched in early spring. Mulches used primarily to protect shrubs and perennials from severe winter cold should be laid down in early winter, when the soil has cooled but not frozen hard; repurposed holiday evergreens are a great material for this. Mulch can be applied anytime in perennial beds and around trees and shrubs.

There are a few circumstances in which it's best to leave the soil uncovered. Don't mulch a low-lying area that's apt to become waterlogged, unless you plan to grow plants adapted to these conditions. Likewise, don't mulch seedlings planted in very moist soils; excessive wetness is an invitation for damping-off, an often fatal fungal disease. Once seedlings are established, it's safe to mulch.

Because organic mulches eventually break down and become part of the soil, mulch must be renewed, usually every two or three years, depending on such factors as climate and the type of mulch you use.

A two- to three-inch layer of bark looks attractive in a perennial bed. Bark is a good option when you need to purchase mulch because it's a recycled by-product of the lumber industry.

Common Organic Mulches

Organic mulches not only discourage the growth of weeds and conserve moisture, they also break down and help enrich the soil, unlike inorganic mulches like crushed stone and plastics. The best mulches are derived from other activities, such as timber operations (for example, bark), agriculture (crop by-products), and home gardening (leaves, pine needles). To conserve energy consumed by long-distance shipping, use mulches produced locally. Following are some commonly available organic mulches and tips on applying and using them.

Shredded Leaves

Application depth: 2 to 3 inches

The big advantage of leaves is that they're readily available in most gardens in the fall. Partially shredded leaves are less likely to mat and shed water than whole leaves, so try to run your rakings through a leaf shredder or pass the lawn mower over them a few times before applying them in beds and around trees and shrubs.

Bark

Application depth: 2 to 3 inches

Bark mulches are widely available and attractive; because they are a recycled by-product of the lumber industry, they're preferable to wood chips, which may be made from trees felled solely for the manufacture of mulch. Look for products expressly labeled "bark mulch," not just wood or hardwood mulch. Shredded bark is more likely to stay in place than nuggets, which can float away in heavy rain.

Wood Chips
Application depth: 3 to 4 inches
Wood chips are commonly available, but avoid mulches made from species of conservation concern, especially cypress. To make sure you aren't purchasing recycled construction and demolition debris contaminated with chromated copper arsenate (CCA), look for products certified by the Mulch & Soil Council. Shredded wood is less likely to float away in downpours than wood chips.

Pine Needles.
Application depth: 4 to 6 inches
If you have pine trees on your property, their needles make a great mulch. They are light and fluffy and don't get compacted, so water penetrates easily. They're best used around acid-loving plants because they tend to lower soil pH.

Nutshells
Application depth: About 2 inches
Pecan shells and other nutshells are not as readily available as other mulch materials, but if they are an agricultural by-product in your area, by all means use them.

They are somewhat more formal looking than other mulches and just as effective at retaining soil moisture. Be aware that cocoa hulls, a by-product of chocolate processing, contain compounds toxic to dogs, so if you have a pooch that likes to dig and chew, this mulch is not for you.

Straw
Application depth: 6 to 8 inches
Use straw, not hay, which usually is full of weed seeds. Although an effective mulch, straw isn't very attractive in perennial planting beds but is fine for the vegetable garden.

Usually available in abundance and cost-free, leaves are a great mulch. If possible, shred them before applying.

Soil Care Strategies

Few gardeners are blessed with "ideal" soil—that deep, well-draining yet moisture-retentive, humus-rich loam celebrated in horticultural literature. Instead, many of us inherit soils that are naturally heavy or sandy, shallow or wet, or that have been altered by human activities. The following pages provide tips for gardening in challenging soil situations. For more information, visit bbg.org/soils.

Gardening in Challenging Conditions

Soil Care Tips for Specific Plants

Acidic Soils

Niall Dunne

What It Is A soil is acidic, or "sour," when its pH is lower than 7, or neutral. See "Understanding Soil pH," page 28.

How It Forms Acidic soils are commonplace in regions with high average rainfall, such as the eastern U.S. Rainwater slowly leaches mineral cations like calcium and magnesium from the soil and replaces them with hydrogen ions, which lowers pH. Other factors that cause acidity include organic matter decomposition, acid rain pollution, and use of ammonium fertilizer.

Challenges Extremely to strongly acidic soils (pH 3.5 to 5.5) are often low in the nutrients calcium, magnesium, and potassium. In addition, they may contain toxic levels of soluble iron, manganese, and—most notably—aluminum. Strongly acidic conditions also reduce bacterial activity in the soil and, consequently, the rate of nutrient release from organic matter.

Sustainable Gardening in Acidic Soils

Most garden plants do best in slightly acidic soil (pH 6.2 to 6.8) but can generally tolerate pH levels as low as 5.5. If your soil pH is much lower than 5.5, the most sustainable solution is to grow adapted plants (see "Plants for Acidic Soils," next page). Another option is to raise the pH using certain amendments. Applying limestone is the traditional solution; however, limestone is a nonrenewable resource, mined from surface quarries, and its production is energy intensive and environmentally destructive. Sustainable gardeners can reduce their reliance upon lime by cutting back on the number of planting beds they amend or by switching to recycled organic amendments.

Liming Adding finely ground limestone (calcium carbonate) gradually neutralizes soil acidity and binds up toxic aluminum. Application rates vary with soil texture. In general, to raise pH by 0.5 points in the top six inches of 100 square feet of clayey soil, six pounds of lime are needed; for loamy soil, add four pounds; for sandy soil, two pounds. For best results, have your soil tested, and follow the recommendations on the report. Changing pH with lime takes time (about a

North American native blueberries thrive in acidic soil conditions.

Applying limestone is the usual way to sweeten acidic soil. Growing adapted plants like sweet woodruff is a more sustainable approach that doesn't require nonrenewable resources.

year), and the effect is only temporary; after a few years, the treatment must be repeated.

Organic Matter Many organic amendments, such as animal manure, legume residues, and wood ash are high in calcium compounds (such as calcium oxide), which raise soil pH. Wood ash also contains high levels of potassium, so use it sparingly to avoid nutrient imbalances; apply no more than two pounds per 100 square feet every two to three years. In addition, most finished composts are close to neutral in pH and can help moderate extreme acidity (or alkalinity) in soils. They can also bind up toxic aluminum and buffer soil against further pH changes. Layer or mix in one to three inches of compost per year.

Plants for Acidic Soils

A selection of plants that do well in strongly acidic soils (pH 4.5 to 5.5). For an expanded list, visit bbg.org/soils.

Trees
Abies species (firs)
Cedrus species (cedars)
Pinus species (pines)
Salix species (willows)

Shrubs
Erica species (heaths)
Kalmia species (mountain laurels)
Myrica species (bayberries)
Rhododendron species (rhododendrons)
Vaccinium species (blueberries)

Perennials
Convallaria majalis (lily-of-the-valley)
Galium odoratum (sweet woodruff)
Gentiana species (gentians)
Lilium species (lilies)
Tiarella cordifolia (foamflower)

Edibles
Foeniculum vulgare (fennel)
Solanum tuberosum (potato)
Rheum × hybridum (rhubarb)

Alkaline Soils

Niall Dunne

What It Is A soil is alkaline, or "sweet," when its pH is higher than 7, or neutral. See "Understanding Soil pH," page 28.

How It Forms Alkaline soils are common in dry to arid regions, such as the western U.S. Here, evaporation exceeds precipitation, and non-acid-forming cations, such as calcium and magnesium, accumulate in the soil rather than leach away. These soils are often rich in carbonates (such as limestone, or calcium carbonate), which dissolve to form hydroxyl ions, increasing alkalinity. Artificial factors raising pH include leaching of lime from concrete in urban areas, over-liming of soil by gardeners, and use of nitrate fertilizers.

Challenges The main problem associated with moderately to strongly alkaline soil (pH 8 to 10) is reduced solubility—and thus availability to plants—of the nutrients phosphorus, iron, zinc, copper, and manganese.

Sustainable Gardening in Alkaline Soils

Many garden plants can tolerate slightly alkaline soil (pH 7 to 8); see "Plants for Alkaline Soils," next page, or contact your botanic garden or native plant society for advice on appropriate local species. If your soil pH tests higher than 8, you can try lowering it using a soil-acidifying amendment. This is difficult in soils with high concentrations of free lime, which creates a buffer against acidification. In these soils, gardening in raised beds is the best solution (see "Raised and Mounded Beds," page 98). To modify highly alkaline soils, choose recycled organic amendments over mined or synthetic ones whenever possible, and avoid fertilizers that raise pH, such as nitrate-based synthetics and wood ash.

Sulfur Incorporating mined elemental sulfur, sometimes called flowers of sulfur, into the soil is the traditional method for lowering pH. Bacteria in the soil slowly convert the sulfur into sulfuric acid, which lowers pH. Application rates vary with soil texture. In general, to lower pH of clayey soils by one point to a depth of six inches, apply 3 pounds of sulfur per 100 square feet; apply 2 pounds of sulfur to loamy soils; and about

Low-growing species and cultivars of phlox make an attractive border for a path made of concrete pavers, which can leach lime and raise the pH of nearby soil.

Many garden plants, such as ground-covering bergenias, tolerate moderately alkaline soils. Raised beds may be the easiest option for gardening in highly alkaline soils.

1¹/₂ pounds to sandy soils. For best results, have your soil analyzed and follow the recommendations on the report. Keep the soil moist during and after application. Test the soil again after a year; if it's not at the desired pH, repeat the application.

Ammonium Sulfate Fertilizer

Nitrifying bacteria in the soil convert ammonium-based synthetic fertilizers into nitrate, water, and hydrogen ions, which lower soil pH. If you use these fertilizers, only do so at rates consistent with recommendations for supplying nutrients to your plants.

Organic Matter Acidic organic materials such as oak leaf mold, compost made from sawdust or other wood by-products, and mulches made from bark or pine needles can be used to gradually lower soil pH—or to maintain it at the desired pH once you've amended with sulfur.

Plants for Alkaline Soils

A selection of plants that do well in slightly alkaline soils (pH 7 to 8). For an expanded list, visit bbg.org/soils.

Trees

Catalpa species (catalpas)
Cercis species (redbuds)
Gleditsia triacanthos (honey locust)
Platanus species (sycamores)

Shrubs

Forsythia species (forsythias)
Kolkwitzia amabilis (beauty bush)
Spiraea species (spireas)
Syringa species (lilacs)

Perennials

Bergenia species (bergenias)
Dianthus species (pinks)
Geum species (avens)
Phlox species (phlox)

Edibles

Asparagus officinalis (asparagus)
Brassica oleracea (cabbage, broccoli)
Beta vulgaris subsp. *cicla* (Swiss chard)

Clayey Soils

Niall Dunne

What It Is In clayey or "heavy" soils, roughly 40 percent or more of the mineral content is composed of clay particles. These tiny particles form tight, dense aggregates with small pore spaces. They also have net negative charges and large surface areas that enable them to hold onto cation nutrients. As a result, soils high in clay are generally quite fertile. See "Texture," page 9.

How It Forms Clays, widespread throughout North America, form from the chemical weathering of minerals such as quartz, feldspars, and micas.

Challenges Because of their small pores, clayey soils are prone to poor drainage and aeration, which can harm or kill many plants and soil organisms. Clayey soils are slow to warm up in spring. When wet, they are sticky and hard to work. They also compact easily, further restricting air and water movement as well as root growth. Wet clayey soils expand and contract during winter freezes and thaws, leading to frost heave and root damage. When they dry out in summer, clays can become hard as cement and impervious to water.

Sustainable Gardening in Clayey Soils

The most sustainable course of action is to select plants that adapt well to heavy soils (see "Plants for Clayey Soils," next page, or contact your botanic garden or native plant society for advice on appropriate local species). Or you can improve soil aeration, drainage, and workability by using conditioners and mulches. When digging in clay, use a spading fork rather than a shovel. Only work clayey soil when it's moist—as opposed to wet or dry—to avoid compacting it or damaging its structure. If you turn over large clods, let them air-dry before crumbling them with a rake. Install pathways in your garden to minimize compaction from foot traffic. Irrigate clayey soils slowly (to make

Thistles do well in clay soils. Before you remove this or other weeds, remember that any plant is better for the soil than no plant at all.

Goldenrods tolerate a range of conditions and offer variety to gardeners: Some species grow to five feet and spread by underground runners, others are petite clumpers that reach barely two feet.

sure the water infiltrates the soil) and infrequently (to avoid waterlogging).

Conditioning Bulky organic conditioners such as finished compost, aged manure, and leaf mold gradually lighten clayey soils by modifying their structure (see "Conditioning Your Soil," page 42). Adding coarse-grained sand also improves aeration and drainage, but sand is a nonrenewable resource, and

you need to apply it in very large amounts (about 50 percent by volume) to see lasting beneficial effects.

Mulching Organic mulches lighten clayey soils as they break down over time. Mulches also make the surfaces of clay-heavy soils more resistant to crusting and compaction and shield them from the baking effects of the sun (see "The Magic of Mulch," page 68).

Plants for Clayey Soils

Following is a selection of plants that tolerate clayey conditions.
For an expanded list of plants, visit bbg.org/soils.

Trees
Acer pensylvanicum (striped maple)
Alnus cordata (Italian alder)
Carpinus betulus (hornbeam)
Malus species (crabapples, apples)
Salix species (willows)

Shrubs
Abelia × grandiflora (glossy abelia)
Ilex crenata (Japanese holly)
Pieris floribunda (mountain pieris)

Viburnum species (viburnums)
Weigela species (weigelas)

Perennials
Aconitum species (monkshood)
Ajuga species (bugle weed)
Bergenia crassifolia (heartleaf bergenia)
Echinacea purpurea (coneflower)
Hemerocallis species (daylilies)
Solidago species (goldenrods)
Symphyotrichum species (asters)

Sandy Soils

Niall Dunne

What It Is In sandy or "light" soils, roughly 70 percent or more of the mineral content is composed of sand particles. Because of the large size of these particles, sandy soils are porous and light to dig. Water infiltrates them readily and drains quickly; air and plant roots penetrate with ease. However, sand particles are chemically inert and so are unable to bind nutrient ions. See "Texture," page 9.

How It Forms Sand is created by the weathering and decomposition of many different kinds of rock, but its most common source is silica (silicon dioxide).

Challenges Sandy soils typically suffer from inadequate water retention and lack of nutrients. Cation exchange capacity is low and drainage is fast, so supplemental nutrients from quick-release fertilizers can leach quickly and contaminate streams and rivers. Sandy soils get hot in the day and cold at night because there is little water present to moderate temperature fluctuations. Because air is abundant, microorganisms decompose organic matter very quickly. If organic matter is in low supply, sandy soils lack structure and may not have enough strength to support the aboveground weight of many plants. Wind erosion is also an issue for dry sandy soils.

Sustainable Gardening in Sandy Soils

The most sensible approach to gardening in sandy soil is to plant drought-tolerant species that adapt well to low-fertility conditions (see "Plants for Sandy Soils," next page, or contact your botanic garden or native plant society for advice on appropriate local species). The more traditional panacea is to add organic matter. This builds structure in sandy soil, improving water and nutrient retention and thus the environment for plant roots. Using water-conservation techniques such as mulching (see "The Magic of Mulch," page 68) is also a must in gardens with sandy soil. When irrigating sandy soils, do so sparingly yet frequently, so plants get the water they need and leaching is minimized. Installing an under-

North American native mountain ash grows best in light, moist, well-draining soils and produces an abundance of persistent red fruit that are devoured by birds in winter.

Drought-tolerant globe thistles grow naturally on gravelly hillsides, making them good candidates for sunny spots with fast-draining sandy soil that's low in organic matter.

ground or drip-irrigation system will help cut down on evaporation of surface water from your garden.

Conditioners Since organic matter decomposes quickly in sandy soils, add a mix of fast- and slow-digesting conditioners. Compost, rotted manure, and grass clippings provide a quick injection of humus into the soil; coarser materials such as sawdust and straw break down more slowly. As they decompose, high-carbon conditioners such as sawdust or bark can draw down soil nitrogen levels, so compost them before use, or add an organic source of supplemental nitrogen. Planting and then tilling under green manures is also a good way to add humus and nitrogen to sandy soils (see "Green Manure," page 66).

Plants for Sandy Soils

Following is a selection of plants that thrive in sandy conditions. For an expanded list of plants, visit bbg.org/soils.

Trees
Cotinus obovatus (American smoke tree)
Gleditsia triacanthos (honey locust)
Koelreuteria paniculata (golden-rain tree)
Pinus strobus (white pine)
Sorbus species (mountain ashes)

Shrubs
Ceanothus × *delileanus* (California lilac)
Cistus species (rock roses)
Rhus species (sumacs)

Perennials
Achillea species (yarrows)
Echinops species (globe thistles)
Gaura lindheimeri (gaura)
Rudbeckia species (coneflowers)

Edibles
Arachis hypogaea (peanut)
Citrullus lanatus (watermelon)
Prunus persica (peach)

Wet Soils

Niall Dunne

What It Is In wet soils—often referred to as poorly draining soils—pore spaces are often filled with water, and soil air can be in short supply.

How It Forms A number of different factors can contribute to wet soil in your garden. A high percentage of clay particles in your soil (see "Clayey Soils," page 82), or a surface or subsurface layer of compaction (see "Compacted Soils," page 92), may be restricting drainage. Other possible causes include a high water table, poor grading, and runoff from buildings and hardscape.

Challenges Without a steady supply of oxygen circulating through the topsoil, most plants and soil organisms can't function properly. A perpetually wet soil can result in suffocation, disease, decline, and eventual death of the roots of many garden plants. In low-oxygen conditions, decomposition of organic matter and nutrient release by soil microorganisms is restricted; moreover, nitrogen may be lost from the soil due to the activity of anaerobic denitrifying bacteria (see "The Nitrogen Cycle," page 33).

Sustainable Gardening in Wet Soils

The most sustainable technique for gardening in wet soil is to plant species that thrive in boggy conditions (see "Plants for Wet Soils," next page, or contact your botanic garden or native plant society for advice on appropriate local species). Planting in raised beds is another low-impact solution (see "Raised and Mounded Beds," page 98).

Managing storm-water runoff is important for soil care as well as for reducing environmental pollution. You can dramatically reduce runoff from your home by installing a green roof. You can also divert rainwater from your drainpipes into an irrigation cistern or directly into a rain garden filled with beautiful wetland plants.

Soil modification is also an option, unless your soggy soil is the result of a high water table. Drainage-impeding layers of compac-

Summersweet grows well in moist soils, and its flowers are a magnet for bees and butterflies.

Deciduous winterberry holly can tolerate the low-oxygen conditions of wet soils.

tion can be broken up, at least temporarily, using a core aerator or other means (see "Compacted Soils," page 92). Applying organic matter is another option for compacted and heavy soils. If you must have a dry garden, you can—as a last resort—hire a contractor to install a drainage system.

Draining the Soil The classic approach to draining wetlands is, of course, to dig a ditch. But drainage ditches in the garden can be unsightly and hazardous (unless filled with an ornamental gravel) and a magnet for mosquitoes. A more sensible solution is to install an underground system of sloped, perforated pipes to drain water into a catchment area, such as a pond, roadside ditch, or dry well. A permit may be required, so contact your local soil conservation service or Cooperative Extension for advice on designing and installing a drainage system.

Plants for Wet Soils

Following is a selection of plants that thrive in wet conditions. For an expanded list, visit bbg.org/soils.

Trees
Betula nigra (river birch)
Nyssa sylvatica (tupelo)
Populus species (cottonwoods)
Salix species (willows)
Taxodium distichum (bald cypress)

Shrubs
Clethra alnifolia (summersweet)
Cornus sericea (red-osier dogwood)
Hamamelis species (witch-hazels)

Ilex verticillata (winterberry holly)
Sambucus canadensis (American elder)

Perennials
Astilbe species (astilbes)
Butomus umbellatus (flowering rush)
Caltha palustris (marsh marigold)
Eupatorium purpureum (Joe-pye weed)
Lobelia cardinalis (cardinal flower)
Salvia uliginosa (bog sage)

Shallow Soils

Niall Dunne

What It Is Shallow soils most often consist of either a thin layer of topsoil covering a dense, clayey subsoil or one covering a rocky or gravelly substrate.

How It Forms Shallow soils with rocky substrate occur naturally in the West and Southwest. Many of the soils in these regions are young and haven't had time to develop deep, distinct layers. Topsoil on hillsides and sloped terrain is generally shallower than on level ground due to erosion by wind and fast-moving surface water (see "Gardening on Slopes," page 99). Shallow soils are also caused by human disturbances. During construction, builders typically remove most or all of the topsoil from a site; construction machinery can also cause serious compaction of the surface soil layers, complicating soil improvement. Erosion due to poor soil management practices—such as overtillage—may also be a factor.

Challenges Shallow soils limit the growth and function of plant roots. Biological activity and organic matter content are low in shallow soils, as are nutrient and water levels. Such soils are difficult to cultivate and plant and also have a tendency to dry out very quickly after watering. Trees growing in them are more susceptible to being blown over during wind storms than trees rooted in deep soil.

Sustainable Gardening in Shallow Soils

If your topsoil is naturally thin, one solution is to grow shallow-rooted, drought-tolerant plants adapted to rocky environments. See "Plants for Shallow Soils," next page, or contact your botanic garden or native plant society for advice on appropriate local species. Creating raised beds with imported topsoil is another option (see "Raised and Mounded Beds," page 98). Soils that have been stripped by human activity can be gradually restored with organic conditioners and mulches. If your budget allows it, you can accelerate the restoration process by trucking in commercial topsoil.

Organic Matter Incorporating organic conditioners such as green manure or coir dust and mulching with organic materials such as shredded leaves or wood chips

Whether formed naturally or by human disturbance, shallow soils are low in organic matter and limit root growth, restricting planting choices to compact, drought-tolerant survivors like sedums.

Chives are one of the few edible plants that thrive in shallow soils.

will help rebuild soil structure and protect your topsoil from further erosion. See "Conditioning Your Soil," page 42, and "The Magic of Mulch," page 68.

Importing Topsoil Commercial topsoil varies in quality. It's generally a "designed" soil mixture, consisting of some salvaged native topsoil and a variety of inorganic and organic materials (such as sand, compost, and manure). It may be contaminated with weeds, salts, herbicides, or garbage. It also may have too much organic matter mixed in, making it a potential source of groundwater contamina-

tion (the optimal level for organic matter in humid climates is about 5 percent by weight, which is reached by adding compost or other organic conditioners at a range of 15 to 20 percent by volume). Make sure to physically inspect it and have it analyzed at a lab before purchasing. To minimize environmental impacts, purchase your topsoil from salvaged rather than harvested sources. Also, before applying new topsoil, you need to make sure that the subsoil drains well. If it's very heavy or compacted, you will need to address this problem first (see "Compacted Soils," page 92).

Plants for Shallow Soils

Following is a selection of shallow-rooted perennials that do well in thin, droughty topsoil. For an expanded list, visit bbg.org/soils.

Allium schoenoprasum (chives)
Allium senescens (German garlic, broadleaf chives)
Aster alpinus (alpine aster)
Campanula rotundifolia (harebell)
Delosperma cooperi (trailing ice plant)
Delosperma nubigenum (yellow ice plant)

Dianthus deltoides (meadow pink)
Jovibarba allionii (house leek)
Orostachys boehmeri (dunce's cap)
Petrorhagia saxifraga (tunic flower)
Sedum species (stonecrops)
Sempervivum species (house leeks)
Talinum calycinum (fameflower)

Saline Soils

Niall Dunne

What It Is Saline soils contain high levels of water-soluble salts, in particular chlorides and sulfates of sodium, calcium, and magnesium. Enough salts may precipitate out of the soil solution to form a white crust at the surface.

How It Forms Some soils, particularly those in dry or arid regions, are naturally high in soluble salts. Rainfall in these regions is low, so salts accumulate in the topsoil rather than leach away. Poor drainage further increases salt accumulation. Saline soils may also form in arid areas due to a high water table: If the soil surface is dry, dissolved salts are pulled up from the groundwater by capillary action. Soils in seaside areas can also be naturally saline due to wind deposition of salt. Salting of roads during icy conditions can lead to salinization of nearby soil. Soil salinity can also be increased artificially by fertilizer application or by irrigating with saline water.

Challenges Too much salt in the soil interferes with a plant's ability to absorb water, resulting in drought stress or wilting. High concentrations of some mineral ions can lead to nutrient disorders—for example, high sodium may cause calcium and potassium deficiency. High levels of sodium can also be toxic to many plants. Though salts are pH neutral, saline soils tend also to be alkaline and may present challenges associated with high pH (see "Alkaline Soils," page 80).

Sustainable Gardening in Saline Soils

Growing salt-tolerant plants is the simplest solution (see "Plants for Saline Soils," next page). In arid regions, mulching helps reduce salt accumulation by reducing surface evaporation. Gardeners with saline soil should avoid amendments that are high in salts (such as langbeinite, fresh manure, and biosolids) or raise soil pH (such as wood ashes). If poor drainage is an issue, you can improve the soil by digging in organic matter that's not high in salt, such as compost. Careful irrigation techniques should be used to avoid evaporation at the surface or saturation of the subsoil—in other words, water frequently but lightly. Soil surfaces can also be leached of excess salts (at

Saline soils with poor drainage can be amended with organic matter such as compost, giving plants like these sunflowers a boost.

Contrary to common gardening advice, plants growing in saline soils like these bee balms should be watered frequently but lightly.

least temporarily) by controlled flooding with large amounts of fresh water; however, this option is only feasible if the soils already drain readily and if large amounts of good-quality (low-salt) irrigation water are available.

Leaching The amount of water needed to remove salts from the root zone will vary according to initial salt levels, soil drainage, desired salt levels, and water quality. A useful rule of thumb is that one unit depth of water will remove 80 percent of salts from the equivalent depth of soil. So, ten inches of water would remove 80 percent of salt present in the top ten inches of soil.

Plants for Saline Soils

Following is a selection of plants that tolerate saline conditions. For an expanded list, visit bbg.org/soils.

Trees
Cercis species (redbuds)
Gleditsia triacanthos (honey locust)
Juniperus species (junipers)
Serenoa repens (saw palmetto)

Shrubs
Clethra species (summersweets)
Forsythia × *intermedia* (forsythia)
Hippophae rhamnoides (sea buckthorn)

Lonicera sempervirens (trumpet honeysuckle)

Perennials
Coreopsis species (coreopsis)
Dianthus species (pinks)
Helianthus species (sunflowers)
Monarda species (bee balms)
Phlox species (phlox)
Symphyotrichum species (asters)

Compacted Soils

Christopher Roddick

You're walking down one of your favorite hiking trails, looking at the clear path though the forest floor ahead of you. And you begin to wonder, "Why is the path so clear, yet mere inches from the edge, the ground is teeming with plant life?" One obvious reason is that any plants attempting to colonize the pathway will get trampled. But that's only part of the story. Keep everybody off the trail for a year or two, and you'll still find very few plants growing on it. That's because compaction has literally squeezed the life out of the soil.

A healthy forest or garden soil is made up of roughly 50 percent pore space, which enables air and water to penetrate through to plant roots and allows excess water to drain away. Compaction occurs when weight bearing down on the soil—from a hiker's boots or a gardener's Wellingtons—causes the larger pore spaces to collapse. The spongy, granular structure of the soil is squeezed into a tight, dense, horizontal barrier that constricts the movement of air and water and limits the growth and expansion of plant roots.

Even if foot traffic along this path stopped, plant life would be limited because over time, countless pairs of pounding feet have squeezed the air out of the topsoil.

Causes and Effects

Compaction is most often associated with human activities such as foot traffic and use of heavy machinery—which is why it's very common in soils surrounding newly constructed houses. But it can also be caused by natural forces such as heavy rainfall, glaciation, and leaching of clay particles into the subsoil. Loss of organic matter also makes soils more susceptible to compaction by weakening their structure. Soils compacted at the surface are prone to flooding during rainstorms and susceptible to droughty conditions since water runs off rather than infiltrates the soil. A compaction layer in the subsoil can cause water-

Often caused by heavy machinery around newly built homes, compaction makes life in the soil difficult, restricting the biological activities of plants and soil-dwelling wildlife alike.

logging and low-oxygen conditions in the root zone because excess moisture is prevented from draining off.

The direct effects of compaction on plants include reduced growth, tip dieback, root rot, and dehydration. But compaction adversely affects plants in a more indirect way as well—by making life difficult for the beneficial organisms that inhabit the soil pores. Just like plant roots, soil microorganisms and arthropods need a balanced supply of air and water to survive and perform their important roles in the soil food web (see "Ecology of the Soil," page 14). Without a community of soil organisms to aerate the soil and turn organic matter into humus—you'll have a hard time growing a healthy, sustainable garden.

Is My Soil Compacted?

There are a number of ways to check for compaction in your soil. The percolation test in "Getting to Know Your Soil," page 34, is a good place to start, because drainage problems may be an indicator of subsoil compaction. A more precise approach is to have your soil's bulk density (the dry weight of a given volume of soil) measured by a qualified soil laboratory, but you need special equipment to collect a sample for it. An easier option is the penetration resistance test, which measures how hard it is to push an object into the soil. Professional landscapers use an instrument called a penetrometer for this test, but home gardeners can perform a rough version of it using a large screwdriver (about one-quarter-inch thick and a foot long). If the screwdriver slides into your soil all the way without much effort, you're probably in good shape. If a moderate amount of force is needed, some compaction may be present, and you should investigate further. If you can't push the screwdriver in at all, or it stops short (and hasn't hit a rock), your soil is most likely compacted. Dry soils are more resistant to penetration than wet ones, so do a few tests at different times to get an average measure for your soil.

You can also detect signs of compaction in your plants. In trees and shrubs, look for stunted growth and dieback or other signs such as wilting, yellowing of leaves, and early fall coloring. In lawns, look for browning out, weeds getting the upper hand over your grass, and increased evidence of fungal disease. Keep an eye on garden perennials for nutrient deficiencies (see "The Essential Minerals," page 30), changes in foliage color, lack of flowering, or wilting. Perennials may have difficulty establishing due to root rot from poor drainage.

One more thing you can do if you suspect a compaction problem is to dig around a bit. If the act of digging itself is difficult, that might be a clue right there. But also examine plant roots as you dig. They should look healthy—moist, well branched, somewhat white or light brown in color—and they shouldn't break off too easily

Core aerators pull up four- to six-inch plugs from garden beds or lawns, allowing air and water access to the root zone.

when tugged. Stunted roots or roots that suddenly veer sideways may indicate lack of air or the presence of a compaction zone, respectively. Smell the soil too: Compacted soils often smell sour (due to anaerobic bacteria) instead of sweet and earthy.

Cures for Compaction

In the long term, the key to repairing a compacted soil is to rebuild its structure. This means replenishing and maintaining the soil's supply of organic matter (roughly 5 percent by weight in humid climate soils) and restoring the organisms that feed on the organic matter—and by doing so, aggregate and aerate the soil. You can accomplish this over time by mixing in compost and other soil conditioners (see "Conditioning Your Soil," page 42) or by top-dressing your soil with good organic mulches (see "The Magic of Mulch," page 68). Spraying microbial compost teas over the mulch may also aid in the process of injecting life back into the soil (see "Compost Tea," page 57).

Simply top-dressing with an inch of good compost will improve lightly to moderately compacted soils: Critters such as earthworms will gradually pull the organic matter into the soil and make it looser and more permeable. A two- to three-inch layer of composted arborist's wood chips or leaf mulch will relieve compaction problems in garden beds and around permanent plantings in much the same way. Mulching also prevents future compaction problems by protecting bare soil from pounding rain.

Physically aerating your soil can also speed up the healing process. One tool often recommended for the job is the broad fork, or U-bar, which looks like a heavy-duty spading fork with very long tines. Basically, you push the fork into the ground, using your body weight, and rock it back and forth to loosen compacted soil. However, I find that U-bars actually increase compaction when you push down on them! I prefer to use a core aerator, which works by pulling four- to six-inch-long plugs from garden beds or lawn areas, allowing air and water access to the root zones of the plants. Aerators vary in size: You can either purchase a small, handheld device or rent a large, walk-behind machine.

To break up really severe compaction layers, you may want to hire a professional landscaper. He or she can perform techniques such as vertical mulching (drilling deep holes in your beds or around your trees and backfilling them with compost) or air trenching (blasting trenches in the soil with a high-pressure air spade and backfilling with compost) to loosen the compaction while minimizing damage to plant roots.

To prevent future compaction, avoid walking on your soil as much as possible, especially when it's wet. Clay soils are more prone to compaction than sandy ones, but all soil types can be damaged. Create pathways so that you can move around or work in the garden without treading on planting beds or over the root zones of trees. Use walls, fences, mulches, or plantings to direct people away from root-zone areas.

Contaminated Soils

Christopher Roddick

We live in a polluted world, and contamination of soil is a major concern in urban, suburban, and rural areas alike. Soil pollutants come from a wide range of sources, including industrial waste, factory emissions, pesticides, car exhaust, deicing salt, and peeling paint. They pose a potential hazard not only to you and your family but also the plants and beneficial organisms in your garden.

Symptoms of poisoning in plants (such as stunted growth and yellowing of foliage) can be hard to distinguish from the symptoms of certain diseases and nutrient deficiencies. The only reliable way to know if there are toxins in your soil is to have it tested. Testing should be done for specific contaminants based on evidence of past contamination. For instance, testing for lead around old houses or adjacent to busy streets is advisable. In areas with mine spoils or downwind of smelters, it makes sense to test soil for heavy metal contaminants such as arsenic, mercury, and lead. Contact your local health department to learn about known contaminated sites and whether or not soils in your neighborhood could be contaminated.

For soils with low levels of contamination, a number of general steps can be taken to manage the problem. For instance, adding organic matter in the form of compost and mulch will bind up contaminants and make them less available in the soil. Blanketing bare ground with mulches or groundcovers will help minimize direct contact between you and the soil. Washing hands after working or playing in the garden and growing produce in contaminant-free containers or raised beds also helps minimize exposure.

If your topsoil is highly contaminated, you should either have it professionally treated or physically removed (and properly disposed of). Contact your state environmental agency for instructions.

Heavy Metals

Heavy metals such as mercury, zinc, lead, and cadmium occur naturally at low levels in the soil, but because of their widespread use in manufacturing, they are increasingly found at toxic levels in the environment. Chronic exposure to heavy metals—either by direct contact or by eating produce grown in contaminated soil—can damage your nervous system and major organs. Most heavy metals, except for lead, are mobile and thus difficult to remove from soils. To reduce their availability for uptake by plants, add organic matter and mulch, keep soil pH close to neutral, and improve soil drainage (oxidizing the metals makes them less soluble).

Lead is the most common heavy metal contaminant in garden soils. The main sources of contamination are lead paint and leaded gasoline, despite the fact that these products were banned decades ago. Unlike other heavy metals, lead is highly immobile and thus very persistent in the environment. Soil adjacent to buildings painted before

Plants can be used to remove toxins from the soil. Under certain conditions, Indian mustard (*Brassica juncea*), shown here, can accumulate high concentrations of lead in its tissues.

the late 1970s or near roadways may still contain toxic levels of lead. More than 300 parts per million of total lead is considered hazardous to children by the Environmental Protection Agency. Plants usually don't absorb large amounts of lead, so the risk is mainly from direct ingestion of contaminated soil or dust. To minimize exposure, follow the general instructions for contaminants and heavy metals above. Also, because lead is so immobile, physically removing the first few inches of soil may rid it of all or most of the contamination.

Pesticides

The overuse or misapplication of herbicides, insecticides, and fungicides can seriously disrupt the soil ecosystem and damage your plants. The risks vary depending on the type of pesticide and the amount applied, as well as other factors. Most modern pesticides are much less persistent than notorious ones like DDT and degrade relatively quickly; nonetheless, their use is strongly discouraged in the sustainable garden. Pesticides used before World War II often contained heavy metals such as arsenic, lead, and copper. Gardens situated on former farms (in particular orchards) should be tested for metal contamination. Testing for modern organic pesticides, however, can be very expensive. There is no one extraction method for all of them, so testing should only be done if there is strong evidence of contamination with a specific compound or compounds. Solutions to pesticide contamination of soils include adding organic matter to reduce the availability of the toxins, and digging in activated charcoal to accelerate the breakdown of pesticide residues.

RAISED AND MOUNDED BEDS
Niall Dunne

A traditional approach to gardening in poor soils is to build a permanent raised bed—basically a box frame or enclosure made of wood, bricks, or concrete blocks and filled with amended topsoil. Raising your native soil above ground level immediately improves internal drainage. An enclosed raised bed also reduces problems associated with conventional beds such as erosion and compaction—foot traffic is eliminated because all management is done from outside the bed.

For growing most vegetables and herbaceous perennials, a raised bed should be at least 8 to 12 inches deep (high). For larger plants, you'll need to build it deeper. Deeper is generally better, because small beds are prone to drying out in summer; however, beds built higher than two feet may need retaining walls, depending on the materials used. You can build your bed as long as your space and irrigation system allows, but don't build it much wider than four feet—so you can maintain it without having to step in. If you build your frame of wood, avoid timber treated with toxic chemicals or creosote.

For soil, you can either amend the native topsoil found under your bed (a traditional mix is one-third native soil, one-third coarse sand, one-third compost) or bring in new topsoil. If you purchase new topsoil, break up the soil underneath the bed before filling it up to avoid creating a drainage barrier. Unless, that is, your garden soil is contaminated—in which case, cover the bottom of the raised bed with a landscape fabric before filling; this will allow air and water movement through the bed but prevent plant roots from accessing the contaminated soil. Once your bed is planted and established, add a layer of compost or aged manure each year to maintain good tilth.

A less formal version of the raised bed is the mounded bed. To build one, mark out

a bed, break up the soil surface, and apply at least a one-foot layer of well-draining topsoil on top. As you work, mold the edges of the bed to create a gently sloping, natural-looking berm—this will help prevent the soil from eroding away with rainfall or irrigation water. Top it all off with a layer of compost or aged manure, let it settle for a week, and start planting.

Raised beds are the cure-all for soil problems, giving you the freedom to mix your own soil.

Gardening on Slopes
Niall Dunne

Steep gradients present a number of challenges to gardeners, not least of which is avoiding taking a spill and rolling down the hill. The biggest problem is soil erosion. Rain and irrigation water move quickly down slopes and—unless there are plants present to stabilize the soil with their roots—wash away the topsoil, leaving behind bare rock or gravel or a thin layer of fast-drying, infertile dirt.

There are a number of ways to cope with a slope. One solution is to plant a mix of low-maintenance groundcovers, shrubs, and trees, making sure to cover any bare patches with mulch or boulders. This layering approach helps stabilize the soil by providing a mix of plant roots at different depths; it also guarantees that falling raindrops have a difficult time scoring a direct hit on the soil surface. And since the plants are easy care, soil disturbance following planting is minimized.

On very steep inclines, you can employ the age-old technique of terracing. Terraces are level planting beds dug into the side of hills and stabilized with retaining walls made of rock, boulders, or brick. They may lack the naturalism and spontaneity of a layered planting, but they can have a pleasing, formal charm. It's also easier to work and amend soils in flat beds in order to grow whatever plants suit your fancy—even rows of vegetables.

More Tips

- Avoid growing and mowing lawn on a steep slope. It's hard work, and grass grown on a hill needs a lot of water.

- Install a drip-irrigation system to minimize water runoff.

- Create a mound of mulch or soil on the downhill side of each plant for water catchment.

- Compost works quite well on slopes if you cover it with a heavier or more permeable mulch such as shredded bark or cocoa bean mulch. Avoid light mulches like straw that are easily stripped off by rain.

Terracing lets you garden in level beds even on steep slopes.

Woody Plants

Christopher Roddick

The key to growing healthy trees and shrubs in the garden is to select species that will adapt well to your climate, space, and soil. Because woody plants—and trees in particular—put out such extensive root systems, it's generally good practice to match them to your soil conditions rather than try to modify your site to meet their needs. It's also more sustainable, because once trees and shrubs are established in an environment closely resembling that of their natural habitat, they should require little maintenance beyond a routine application of good-quality organic mulch.

Familiarize yourself with the growing conditions in your garden. They may vary in different areas. Along with such factors as soil moisture, pH, and volume (the larger the plant, the bigger the root zone), you'll need to take into account light conditions, your USDA hardiness zone, and (for large trees and shrubs) spatial constraints. To find out which tree species will thrive at your garden site,

consult with local nurseries and public gardens for ideas. Most woody plants prefer moist, well-drained, slightly acidic soils, but you can find a broad selection of trees and shrubs that will tolerate almost any situation—even the shallow, compacted, drought-prone soils common in highly disturbed urban sites.

The long-term well-being of a young tree or shrub depends on proper planting techniques. Dig a hole three to five times the diameter of the root-ball or nursery container and just deep enough to accommodate the roots. Remove the container or any wire or burlap surrounding the roots, and place the plant in the center of the hole. Make

Set the tree in its hole and backfill with the soil that you dug up, then water and top-dress with compost.

sure the trunk flare lies above ground level. Backfill the hole with the soil that you dug up and water the plant slowly and deeply. Avoid amending the backfill with organic matter, as this can discourage the roots from growing out into the native soil and cause the soil to subside, or sink. Instead, top-dress the soil with an inch of compost followed by a three-inch layer of coarse organic mulch.

Supplemental watering is crucial to newly transplanted trees for the first season or two, especially in the summer months and during long dry periods in spring or fall. Drench the soil with at least an inch of water any week of summer in which it doesn't rain. Keep an eye out for drought

A two- to three-inch layer of organic mulch is beneficial for most trees. Cover as much of the root zone as possible.

stress, but also be careful not to overwater; if the top three inches of soil don't dry out after a day, discontinue watering.

Most woody plants benefit greatly from a layer of organic mulch. Wood chips or shredded leaves are good options; besides providing all the usual benefits of mulches, they will help build populations of beneficial fungi in the soil. Cover as much of the root zone as you can to a depth of two to three inches. Keep mulch away from the bases of trees and shrubs to prevent disease and rodent damage.

In general, established trees or shrubs that are mulched every year or two with good-quality organic matter won't need supplemental fertilization. If your plants start showing signs of nutrient deficiency—and a soil test confirms that the soil is deficient—spread compost fortified with an appropriate organic or mineral supplement in spring (raking away any mulch first and reapplying it afterward). Avoid nitrate-based fertilizers, which can raise soil pH and create unfavorable conditions for tree roots.

During autumn mulching, be careful not to cover the aboveground crowns of perennials like sedums to avoid the promotion of rot.

Perennials

Niall Dunne

The mantra of sustainable garden design is to select plants (especially natives) that will adapt well to your site conditions—your climate, available light, and soil. With a little sleuthing online or at your local nursery, botanic garden, perennial plant society, or library, you can find wonderful herbaceous perennials for just about any kind of soil. (See also "Gardening in Challenging Conditions," page 78.)

It has to be said, however, that most traditional garden perennials prefer the proverbial moist, well-drained, mildly acidic, moderately fertile, humus-rich soil. If you already have this type of soil in your garden, then you can just start planting. Add an inch or two of compost or aged manure each year in the fall or spring to help maintain adequate nutrient levels and soil structure. And top that off with a layer of coarser organic mulch, such as wood chips, to enhance weed suppression and moisture conservation.

If your soil is sandy, clayey, wet, or compacted—or a soil test reveals nutrient deficiencies or extreme pH—then it's a good idea to prepare the bed before planting. Digging in an organic conditioner such as compost will help solve most problems related to soil texture, drainage, or pH. Amending to a depth of eight inches is generally adequate for most herbaceous perennials. As you work, mix in any necessary nutrient supplements (adequate levels of phosphorus and potassium are particularly important for good plant establishment). Plant your perennials, and mulch as described above.

When mulching, don't cover the aboveground crowns of such plants as peonies (*Paeonia* species and cultivars), sedums (*Sedum*), and columbines (*Aquilegia*), or the foliage of evergreen perennials like pinks (*Dianthus*) and heucheras (*Heuchera*). In established perennial beds top-dressed with compost or manure each year, supplemental nutrients are usually unnecessary. Some perennials, such as dahlias (*Dahlia*) and bleeding hearts (*Dicentra*) are considered heavy feeders and may benefit from an extra dose of balanced organic fertilizer each spring. However, other perennials such

as yarrows (*Achillea*), clematis (*Clematis*), sages (*Salvia*), and daylilies (*Hemerocallis*) are light feeders, and they respond poorly to extra fertilization (growing leggy and toppling over)—one reason, among many, to be careful when it comes to nutrient supplements. A winter mulch of coniferous prunings (for example, from spent holiday greens) can help insulate tender or newly planted perennials in the dormant season. Remove them in early spring before active growth starts. See also "The Magic of Mulch," page 68.

Like these lupines, most perennials require little more soil care than an annual topdressing of compost and a weed-suppressing, moisture-conserving layer of mulch.

Roses

Anne O'Neill

Roses like to have their faces in the sun, the air moving through their leaves, and their roots in cool, fertile, well-drained soil. Early books on rose cultivation were very much focused on soil: They promised healthy plants, abundant flowers, and vibrant colors—all as a direct result of good care of the earth. Then came the era of extreme rose breeding, in which sprays and artificial fertilizers were wielded to produce incredible flowers, and soil became a mere footnote. Today, as gardeners have discovered the true costs of chemical gardening, we are seeing a return to wiser ways—which, in the case of roses, means growing climate-appropriate and disease-resistant cultivars in naturally fertile, biologically active soil.

In the historic Cranford Rose Garden at Brooklyn Botanic Garden, I follow a planting method that I learned in my youth. First, I only plant when the soil is crumbly (damp but not wet) in order to protect its structure. I dig a very wide and appropriately deep hole and put approximately three inches of well-rotted manure

in the bottom of it. After that, I amend the soil from the hole with more manure and drop several inches of it back in the hole and tamp it down. (Note: Amending the backfill soil with organic matter is not recommended when planting large shrubs or trees; see "Woody Plants," page 100). I place the rose in the hole, carefully spread out the roots, water them, add the remainder of the amended soil, tamping gently to make sure that there are no air pockets, and water again. Finally, I spread an inch or so of mulch around the planting, making sure it doesn't touch the canes.

Protect the delicate roots of roses with mulch, but keep it away from the stems to avoid creating cozy homes for hungry munchers.

To protect the health of your soil, choose roses that match the conditions of your garden and will grow well without the use of chemical fertilizers or pesticides.

The benefits of mulching to the soil ecosystem are cumulative over the years and cannot be overstated. I prefer to use precomposted mulches and manure-rich mulches rather than high-carbon (woody) mulches, which may temporarily draw down soil nitrogen levels as they decompose (however, see "The Magic of Mulch," page 68). Though not quite as effective as other mulches at suppressing weeds, compost and manure do an excellent job of moderating moisture levels and temperature extremes in the soil, while also providing a balanced source of essential nutrients as they are incorporated into the soil. I spread about one inch of spent mushroom compost in spring, immediately after pruning the roses. When winter has finally settled in here in New York, I like to protect the roses by mounding them with partially composted leaves, mulching the soil with well-aged manure, and covering the more tender plants with pine branches. My motto has always been this: Be kind to your soil, and it will return the favor by allowing your roses to establish the deep, strong root systems they need for healthy long lives.

Site preparation is crucial for establishing a deep-rooted lawn that requires minimal watering and maintenance and thrives without the application of soil- and water-polluting chemicals.

Lawns

Ronald C. Smith

Most books on sustainable gardening will tell you that one of the most important steps you can take to make your garden more environmentally friendly is to reduce the size of your lawn—or even eliminate it altogether. While it's true that America's obsession with expansive, perfectly manicured lawns has led to many unsustainable practices (including heavy water usage and overuse of chemical fertilizers and pesticides), it is also true that lawns can provide a water-permeable and wear-resistant area for kids, pets, and adults to play and that you can grow an attractive, low-maintenance lawn that's truly "green." The way to do it is to plant a mix of tough, regionally appropriate grasses and take good care of your soil.

Good drainage is a must for establishing a healthy, deeply rooted lawn that can efficiently mine the soil for water and nutrients and resist such stresses as drought, disease, and compaction. The best time to address drainage is before you plant your lawn. Proper grading of the subsoil is ideal. This includes gently sloping the subsoil away from buildings and filling in low-lying areas. You have to temporarily remove the topsoil to adjust the rough grade. If this is not feasible, then at least adjust the surface grade by rotary tilling the topsoil and using the back of a rake to create a slope. Tilling will also loosen the soil and enable you to clear the site of sod or debris.

If your soil is predominately heavy clay, adding organic matter will also improve drainage (see "Clayey Soils," page 82). But before amending your soil, have it tested at a qualified lab. Of all the components measured, phosphorus, potassium, and organic matter are the most important for lawn grasses. A pH range of 6.5 to 7.5 is desirable for optimal nutrient availability, but the importance of pH for lawns may be overstated; I have seen turfgrass grow satisfactorily in soils ranging from 5 (strongly acid) to 8.9 (strongly alkaline).

If your test shows low levels of phosphorus or potassium, then rake some renewable organic sources of these nutrients (see "The Essential Minerals," page 30) into the upper two to four inches of topsoil. The organic matter content of the topsoil should be between 3 and 5 percent. Digging in a layer of compost is the best way to increase organic matter in the topsoil during site preparation. It will feed beneficial soil organisms, improve cation exchange capacity, soil structure (and thus air and water flow), and provide a slow-release form of nitrogen to your lawn.

Once all your amendments are incorporated, rake the soil smooth and then sow your seed. Early fall is the ideal time in most areas, giving seedlings time to develop strong root systems that give them a head start on the following year's growing season. Plant a mix of grasses in your lawn instead of a monoculture. The diversity will increase your lawn's resistance to pests and weeds, helping decrease the need for maintenance. For recommendations on grass species and cultivars that perform well in your area—and for the best times to plant these grasses—contact your county Cooperative Extension. Brooklyn Botanic Garden's handbook *Easy Lawns* provides instructions on how to establish an easy-care lawn using grasses native to your region.

After sowing is done, rake the surface to cover the seeds with about half an inch of soil, and then roll the area. Spread a thin layer of straw mulch, and lightly water the soil several times a day until seedlings emerge. Then gradually reduce watering. Avoid walking on the grass or mowing it for at least a month after sowing.

As the grass matures and proper maintenance is provided, the need to water or fertilize subsides significantly. Proper maintenance includes simple tasks such as mowing the grass high—in general, let it grow to $2^1/_2$ to 3 inches and then trim the top third—and allowing the clippings to remain on the lawn. If fertilizer is needed, spread an organic lawn blend in fall. In time, a modest thatch layer will build up. If it gets no thicker than half an inch, it will benefit your grass. Core aerating (see "Compacted Soils," page 92) every other year will keep the thatch thickness in that range.

Old, poorly maintained lawns typically suffer from compaction, along with buildup of thatch. Compaction and excessive thatch reduce soil aeration and drainage and lead to poor grass growth and density, which in turn sets the stage for weed competition and disease development. Again, core aeration will relieve or greatly reduce these problems. It is best carried out in the early spring, after active growth has begun. Aerating any earlier will give weeds a competitive advantage.

Annuals

Caleb Leech

Our palette of ornamental annuals diversifies with each new season. Gardeners are now using tender perennials and tropicals along with old-fashioned annual favorites to add season-long color to their borders and beds. And it's not unusual to see familiar characters from our kitchen gardens—such as ruby-red chard and ornamental peppers—being used to add visual interest. While annuals have traditionally been viewed as an undemanding group of plants, these recent trends are changing the dynamic somewhat, and gardeners need to be a little more conscientious about managing the fertility of their soil.

Most annuals do best in full sun and moist, well-draining, humus-rich soil with a pH ranging between 5.8 and 7.5. If you have heavy, sandy, or compacted soil, it's a good idea to improve tilth by working in a few inches of organic matter the first year that you prepare your planting bed. Annuals are generally shallow-rooted, so deep digging is unnecessary, unless perhaps your garden has drainage issues resulting from compaction. Once the initial conditioning is done, you should be fine applying an organic mulch such as compost in subsequent years to maintain good soil structure. Worms and other soil organisms will dig the organic matter in for you.

When it comes to growing annuals, many gardeners routinely add soluble fertilizers to the soil throughout the growing season. This approach may have the desired effect of producing fabulous, long-lasting flowers, but it's not sustainable in the long run and may lead to pollution of the environment. Creating a naturally fertile, bio-

Some popular annuals like impatiens, petunias, and zinnias, shown here, take a break from flowering in hot weather and should not be fertilized during that time.

Frost-sensitive snail flower vine is an attractive legume that enriches the soil by capturing nitrogen from the soil air and transforming it into mineral form ready for uptake by roots.

logically active soil can eliminate the need for nutrient supplements. Top-dressing with compost or aged manure each year before sowing or after transplanting will help you accomplish this. If a soil test detects nutrient deficiencies, you can incorporate the appropriate organic amendments into your compost before application.

Another great way to increase nutrient levels in your soil without resorting to packaged fertilizers is to plant nitrogen fixers. Many beautiful annual legumes such as sweet pea (*Lathyrus odoratus*), lupines (*Lupinus* species), and snail flower (*Vigna caracalla*) foster symbiotic bacteria in their roots that capture nitrogen from the atmosphere and transform it into usable mineral form. Others legumes such as crimson clover (*Trifolium incarnatum*) make excellent cover crops for annual beds. A fall planting will protect the otherwise bare bed from erosion through the winter, prevent nutrients from leaching away, and add nitrogen to the soil for next year's plants. It will even provide a nice flush of red color when it blooms in spring. However, clover can be weedy, so be sure to turn it under before the flowers go to seed.

Successful annual borders are never static creations. Modify the design and the content of your border over the years to avoid nutrient depletion of the soil and weed problems. And have fun exploring the colorful world of annual plants!

Vegetables

Greg and Pat Williams

Growing and eating your own food—and sharing your surplus—is a great way to make your garden and lifestyle more sustainable. It saves on the environmental costs of shipping, packaging, and storing food produced in a distant place. And as any kitchen gardener will tell you, homegrown vegetables taste a whole lot better!

In terms of soil care, vegetable gardening is generally more high maintenance than ornamental gardening because (1) harvesting plants results in a net loss of nutrients from the soil; (2) many popular vegetables such as broccoli, lettuce, and corn are "heavy feeders" and have high nitrogen demands; (3) the soil is subject to frequent disturbance, so its organic matter tends to break down quickly; and (4) vegetable growing cycles can leave large areas of a garden periodically uncovered, exposing the soil to rain and wind erosion. But with these challenges come unique opportunities to replenish and improve your soil in a sustainable manner.

Soil care recommendations for sustainable vegetable gardening vary tremendously. Some books advise deep or double digging, while others recommend no digging at

all; some advocate continuous application of mulch, and others suggest tilling in organic material; and some prescribe all kinds of amendments and fertilizers, while others say all you need is compost. Despite the wide spectrum of opinions, most experts do agree on two basic principles: first, that you need to add generous amounts of organic matter regularly to your soil, and second, that the soil surface should be kept covered as much as possible to minimize erosion and compaction.

Neither of these principles is adhered to by growing vegetables in the "traditional" way—that is, tilling the entire vegetable garden in early spring, successively planting in

Whether it makes sense to dig or till your vegetable beds depends on the quality of the soil, the kind of plants you want to grow—and your time.

single rows with wide paths between the rows, controlling weeds by repeated cultivation between the rows, tilling in spent plants, and then leaving the soil bare over the winter. This type of veggie garden might look tidy, but its soil surface is exposed to the elements for long periods, and the repeated tillage damages the soil's structure and food web.

So what should you do in your vegetable garden? If the plot is small, then permanent beds make sense. Whether the beds should be dug or not depends on the quality of the soil, the kind of plants currently growing there, and your available time and physical constraints. If your soil is already a rich, well-draining loam with plant cover that can be easily removed, experiment with minimal digging. By adding compost and mulch only on the soil surface, you mimic nature's soil-building processes and avoid disturbing beneficial soil organisms.

But if your soil is heavy clay, poor-quality compacted builder's fill, or old agricultural soil that has been subjected to repeated cultivation and agrichemicals, loosening the soil at the start of each season by digging or deep tilling will enhance air and water movement, as well as vegetable root growth. Mixing in plenty of organic matter will improve poor or compacted soil more quickly than just spreading organic matter on the surface. In any case, beds should be kept mulched, especially over the winter.

If you are trying to grow lots of vegetables in a large garden, planting at least some of your garden in rows and using a tiller to prepare the soil and keep weeds down might be more practical than beds. (The alternative method of continuous mulching for soil care and weed control would require massive amounts of material for a large garden.) There are several things you can do to minimize the long-term damage to soil structure caused by the tiller. Only till areas of the garden that you're going to plant soon—instead of tilling it all at once. Reduce tillage between rows—it's okay to have some weeds in your garden, especially later in the season, when vegetables can compete fairly well against weeds. Plant any bare areas with green manure crops—the most practical sources of organic matter and fertility for large gardens. Green manures are especially important for winter cover (see "Green Manure," page 66).

Have the soil in your vegetable garden tested every couple of years or so. If nutrient deficiencies are detected, supplement your organic matter application with the appropriate organic fertilizers in spring. In healthy, nutritionally balanced soil, yearly additions of compost or aged manure should replenish minerals removed during harvesting of crops. However, if you grow a lot of heavy feeders such as corn, potatoes, beets, or broccoli, you may need to provide an extra boost of fertilizer. (In large gardens, rotating heavy feeders with nitrogen-fixing cover crops will help cut down on the need for nutrient supplements.) To maximize the availability of the nutrients to your vegetables, keep the pH of your soil between around 5.5 and 7.

For More Information

GENERAL SOIL SCIENCE

The Nature and Properties of Soils
Nyle C. Brady and Ray R. Weil
Pearson/Prentice Hall, 2008

USDA Natural Resources
Conservation Service Soil Site
soils.usda.gov

SOIL ANALYSIS

Alternative Soil-Testing Labs
(organic fertilizer recommendations, soil
food web evaluations, and more)
attra.org/attra-pub/soil-lab.html

COMPOSTING

Urban Composting
bbg.org/composting

Cornell University Composting
compost.css.cornell.edu/
  Composting_Homepage.html

URBAN SOILS

Urban Soils: Applications and Practices
Philip J. Craul
John Wiley & Sons, 1999

USDA NRCS Urban Soils Site
(see especially *Urban Soil Primer*)
soils.usda.gov/use/urban/

ORGANIC SOIL CARE

Improving the Soil
Erin Hynes
Rodale Press, 1994

Start with the Soil
Grace Gershuny
Rodale Press, 1993

SOIL CONSERVATION

Dirt: The Erosion of Civilizations
David R. Montgomery
University of California Press, 2007

Great Lakes Worm Watch
(forest ecology and worms)
nrri.umn.edu/worms

The Soil and Water Conservation Society
www.swcs.org

SOIL ECOLOGY FOR GARDENERS

BLM National Science and
Technology Center
(soil biological communities)
www.blm.gov/nstc/soil/

Life in the Soil:
A Guide for Naturalists and Gardeners
James B. Nardi
University of Chicago Press, 2007

Soil Foodweb, Inc.
soilfoodweb.com

Teaming with Microbes:
A Gardener's Guide to the Soil Food Web
Jeff Lowenfels and Wayne Lewis
Timber Press, 2006

USDA NRCS Soil Biology Primer
soils.usda.gov/sqi/concepts/soil_biology/
  biology.html

NO-TILL GARDENING

Organic Gardening:
The Natural No-Dig Way
Charles Dowding
Green Books, 2007

MATCHING PLANTS TO SOIL/ SITE CONDITIONS

Perfect Plant, Perfect Place
Roy Lancaster
DK Publishing, 2002

Right Plant, Right Place
Nicola Ferguson
Fireside, 2005

Trees in the Urban Landscape: Site
Assessment, Design, and Installation
Peter J. Trowbridge and Nina L. Bassuk
John Wiley & Sons, 2004

BBG BOOKS ON RELATED TOPICS

Easy Compost, 2001
Natural Disease Control, 2000
Natural Insect Control, 1994

To read excerpts from these and other titles,
visit bbg.org/handbooks. To order books,
go to shop.bbg.org or call 718-623-7286.

For additional soil resources, see bbg.org/soils.

112 • HEALTHY SOILS FOR SUSTAINABLE GARDENS

Contributors

Sina Adl is an associate professor in the Department of Biology at Dalhousie University, in Halifax, Canada. He is the author of *The Ecology of Soil Decomposition*, as well as book chapters, reviews, and research papers on soil ecology. His current interests are in soil food web function and soil protist diversity.

Craig Cogger is a research and extension soil scientist at Washington State University, in Puyallup, Washington. He received his PhD in soil science from Cornell University. His research interests include organic nutrient management, organic farming systems, and the use of animal manure, biosolids, and composts in agriculture and urban landscapes. He has written numerous journal articles and more than 30 extension publications and has taught soils classes for master gardeners for more than 20 years.

Niall Dunne is a former editor of Brooklyn Botanic Garden's *Plants & Gardens News* and *Urban Habitats*. He holds an MA in English from University College Dublin and an MS in ecology and evolution from Rutgers University. He currently lives in Seattle and manages publications for the Arboretum Foundation at Washington Park Arboretum.

Grace Gershuny is internationally known in the organic agriculture movement, having worked for over 30 years as an organizer, educator, author, and consultant, as well as a market gardener. She has written extensively on soil management and composting, including *Start with the Soil* and *Compost, Vermicompost, and Compost Tea*. Currently working as a consultant to the organic industry, Grace lives, gardens, and composts in Barnet, Vermont.

Caleb Leech is the curator of the Herb Garden and Hardy Fern Collection at Brooklyn Botanic Garden. He began gardening as a child and today focuses on community gardens, shared landscapes, and the connections people feel with plants and place.

Ulrich Lorimer is the curator of the Native Flora Garden at Brooklyn Botanic Garden. He holds a degree in landscape horticulture from the University of Delaware, has perpetually soiled hands, is an admitted plantaholic, and tries to be outside as much as possible.

Janet Marinelli, former director of Publications at Brooklyn Botanic Garden, is an award-winning author of numerous articles and several books on plants and gardening, including *Stalking the Wild Amaranth* and most recently, the BBG handbook *The Wildlife Gardener's Guide*. She has a particular interest in imperiled plants and what gardeners and other nature lovers can do to help them survive in this age of extinction. You can find out more about Janet and read her blog at janetmarinelli.com.

Stephanie Murphy heads the Rutgers Soil Testing Lab, in New Brunswick, New Jersey. She has a PhD in soil biophysics from Michigan State University, an MS in soil management and conservation from Purdue University, and a BS in agronomy from Ohio State University. Her research interests include soil management, quality, and conservation.

Anne O'Neill is curator of the Shakespeare Garden and Fragrance Garden and the former curator of the Cranford Rose Garden at Brooklyn Botanic Garden.

Sarah Reichard is an associate professor at the University of Washington, Seattle. Her research interests encompass the intersection of conservation biology and horticulture, including invasive plants, rare plant reintroduction to the wild, and sustainable horticultural practices.

Christopher Roddick is an ISA-certified arborist at Brooklyn Botanic Garden. Formerly the head arborist at Scott Arboretum, in Swarthmore, Pennsylvania, he is currently a tree consultant and instructor specializing in mature tree preservation, pruning, and tree diagnostics. He is the coauthor (with Beth Hanson) of the BBG handbook *The Tree Care Primer*.

Ronald C. Smith is an extension horticulture specialist at North Dakota State University, in Fargo, North Dakota. He has an MS in horticultural soil analysis from the University of Georgia and a PhD in landscape horticulture from Ohio State University. He has taught at university level for more than three decades and has worked in horticulture-related industry for ten years.

Pat and Greg Williams have applied their MIT engineering training to food gardening experiments on their farm in central Kentucky for over 30 years. They are regular contributors to BBG's *Plants & Gardens News* and have published their monthly gardening newsletter *HortIdeas* (users.mikrotec.com/~gwill) since 1984.

Photos

Catherine Anstet pages 10, 42, 55, 63, 76, 92, 99, 100
Laura Berman cover, pages 2, 5 (and back cover), 6, 8, 11, 24, 33, 38 (3), 40, 41, 44, 50, 56 (2), 58, 70, 71, 75, 79, 80, 81, 82, 83, 85, 88, 90, 91, 93, 97, 98, 105, 106, 108, 110
Tris Bucaro page 102
Chris Campbell page 9
David Cavagnaro page 30, 64, 66, 68, 84, 86, 87, 89, 101, 109
FPM CO, LTD. page 48
Bill Johnson page 27
Brian Kilford pages 14, 22
Martin LaBar page 104
Christian Mac Kay Tepper page 31
Jason Molinari page 32
Jerry Pavia pages 13, 23, 52, 72, 74, 78, 103
Barry Rice page 49
Neil Soderstrom pages 16, 19, 28, 34 (and back cover), 37, 39 (and back cover), 46, 47, 60, 73, 94

Illustrations

Elizabeth Ennis

Index

fixation of, 15, 30, 33, *33*
importance/sources of, 30
leaching of, 30–31, 61
nitrate (NO_3), 27, 30, 33
Nutrients. *See also* fertilizers *and specific nutrients*
after seeding/transplanting, 64
CEC, 26, *26*
deficiencies/imbalances in, 27–28, 90
factors in availability of, 25–26
macronutrients, 27, 30–32
micronutrients, 32, 53, 58, 62, 65
from organic matter, 7
reserved in subsoil, 12
soil testing for, 27, 38–40, *38–40*
Nutshells, 72, 75

O

Oats, 67
O horizon (soil layer), 12
Organic growing and biosolids, 46
Organic matter, 7–8. *See also* ecology of soil and *specific types of matter*
for acidic soils, 78–79
for aeration, 7
for alkaline soils, 81
for annuals, 108
in biosolids, 46
CEC affected by, 26
climate's effects on, 13, 25
contaminants bound up by, 96–97
decomposition of, 15–17, *25*
in forests, 69
for lawns, 107
pesticides reduced by, 97
for saline soils, 90
for shallow soils, 89, *89*
soil structure improved by, 11, 15, *15*, 21
Organic vs. mineral soils, 7
Organisms in soil. *See* ecology of soil *and specific organisms*

P

Paint, pollution from, 96
Parent material, 13
Peanut hulls, 72
Peat moss, 7, 45, *46*, 48–49, *48, 49*
Pecan shells, 72, 75
Peds. *See* aggregates
Penetrometers, 93
Percolation test (drainage), 37, *37*
Perennials
for acidic soils, 79
for alkaline soils, 81
for clayey soils, 83
compost for, 56
conditioning soil for, 44–45
and cover crops, 65
mulch for, 73, 75
root rot in, 94

for saline soils, 91
for sandy soils, 85
for shallow soils, 89
soil requirements of, 102–103, *102–103*
soil testing for, 40
for wet soils, 87
Perlite, *46*, 47
Pesticides, 16–17, 96–97
Pests, 21–22
Pet safety, and mulch, 75
Petunias, *108*
pH. *See also* acidic soils; alkaline soils
best range, 29, *29*
defined, 28
for lawns, 107
neutral, 22
and nutrient availability, 26
soil test for, 38–40, *38–40*
understanding/testing, 28–29, *28–29*
Phosphate rock, 61
Phosphorus (P), 27–29, 31, 64, 80, 107
Physical properties of soil, 5, 7–13, 36–37. *See also* knowing your soil; structure of soil; texture of soil
Phytophthora root rot, 30
Pine needles, 71, 75
Platy soil structure, 11
Plywood, pressure-treated, 53
Pollen, 49
Pollution, 86, 96, 108. *See also* contaminated soils
Potassium (K), 27–28, 31, 90, 107
Potato (*Solanum tuberosum*), 79, 111
Pressure-treated lumber, 53, 71–72, 75
Primary saprotrophs, 16. *See also* bacteria; fungi
Probiotic compost tea, 23, 41, 57, 60, *94*
Problem soils, 5. *See also* compaction; contaminated soils; soil care strategies for challenging conditions
Proteins, 21, 33
Protists, 17
Protozoa, *18*, 22, 41
Purple pitcher plant, *49*

R

Rain gardens, 86
Raised beds, 5, 43, 80, 86, 88, 98, *98*
Rhizobia (bacteria), 33, 67
Rhizosphere, 19
R horizon (soil layer), 12
Rock phosphate/powders, 53, 60, 64–65
Rodent damage, 101
Roots
erosion prevented/reduced by, 10

hairs of, 20, *20*
and mycorrhizae, 17, 20, *20*
nitrogen's effects on, 30
organisms' interaction with, 19–20, *20*
parasites of, 21
pioneer cells of, 19
respiration by, 8
root rot, 30, 93–94
stubby brown, 32
stunted, 31
water absorbed by, 8
Roses, 104–105, *104, 105*
Rotary tillers, 45, 106
Rotating crops, 22
Roundworms. *See* nematodes
Rubber mulch, 70
Runoff control, 86, 99
Rusts, 16
Rye/ryegrass, 67

S

Saline soils, 44, 90–91, *90–91*
Salt, 96
Sampling, 39–40, *39–40*. *See also* testing of soils
Sand
for drainage/conditioning, 47, 82–83
sample of, *46*
size of particles, 9, *9*
Sandy soils
causes/challenges of, 84
CEC in, 26, *26*
vs. clayey soils, 9
color of, *38*
defined, 84
mulch for, 73
plants for, *84–85*, 85
sulfur for, 80
sustainable gardening in, *84*, 84–85
texture of, 9–10, 35–36, *35–36*
water-/nutrient-holding capacity of, 9
Saprotrophs, 16. *See also* bacteria; fungi
Sawdust, 44, 53
Seaweed, 31, 53, 65
Seed meals, 61, 65
Seeds preserved in sphagnum bogs, 49
Shallow soils, 88–89
Shrubs
for acidic soils, 79
for alkaline soils, 81
for clayey soils, 83
compaction indicators in, 94
compost for, 56, 101
conditioning soil for, 44
mulch for, 73
planting, 100–101, 104
for saline soils, 91
for sandy soils, 85